Baby James Brown

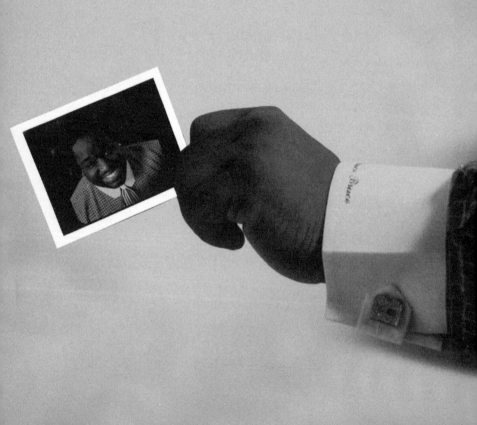

BRUCE BRUCE

Baby James Brown

Roadside Amusements
Published by Chamberlain Bros.
An imprint of Penguin Group (USA) Inc.
New York

ROADSIDE AMUSEMENTS
an imprint of
CHAMBERLAIN BROS.
Published by the Penguin Group
Penguin Group (USA) Inc., 375 Hudson Street, New York, New York 10014, USA
Penguin Group (Canada), 90 Eglinton Avenue, Suite 700, Toronto, Ontario M4P 2Y3,
Canada (a division of Pearson Penguin Canada Inc.)
Penguin Books Ltd, 80 Strand, London WC2R 0RL, England
Penguin Ireland, 25 St Stephen's Green, Dublin 2, Ireland
(a division of Penguin Books Ltd)
Penguin Group (Australia), 250 Camberwell Road, Camberwell, Victoria 3124, Australia
(a division of Pearson Australia Group Pty Ltd)
Penguin Books India Pvt Ltd, 11 Community Centre, Panchsheel Park,
New Delhi–110 017, India
Penguin Group (NZ), Cnr Airborne and Rosedale Roads, Albany, Auckland 1310,
New Zealand (a division of Pearson New Zealand Ltd)
Penguin Books (South Africa) (Pty) Ltd, 24 Sturdee Avenue, Rosebank,
Johannesburg 2196, South Africa

Penguin Books Ltd, Registered Offices: 80 Strand, London WC2R 0RL, England

Library of Congress Cataloging-in-Publication Data

Bruce, Bruce, date.
Baby James Brown / Bruce Bruce.
p. cm.
ISBN 1-59609-037-5 (pbk.)
1. Bruce, Bruce, date.   2. Comedians—United States—Biography.   I. Title.
PN2287 B725 A3 2005   2005050407
792.702'8'092—dc22
[B]

Printed in the United States of America
1 2 3 4 5 6 7 8 9 10

Book design by Elke Sigal

Acknowledgments

To my family and friends, thank you for the love and support. To my boyz, Jimmy Holmes, and Black Boy, who keep my tour life tight; to Team Bruce at Thruline Entertainment (Ron, JB, and Chris) and to my publicist, Jenneifer Patterson—"straight-up-snitch." To Scott Simpson, Steve Levine, Brian Bunin, and all the staff at ICM; Nick Nuciforo and all the staff at APA and my attorney, William Sobel, thanks for the opportunities and for watching my back. And to Adam Williamson, I thank you for your continued belief in me and for the honesty in which you conduct business on my behalf. To Jeanette and Gracie for keeping Adam grounded. A special thanks to Arthur Spivak and all of the staff at Spivak Entertainment, it's been an incredible ride.

To Carlo De Vito, my editor at Chamberlain Bros., great working with you. A very special thanks to James Napoli for your guidance, direction, and input. Also to Walter Latham,

Acknowledgments

you kept me busy and respected. To Jeff Clannagan, Steve Sussman, Komeka Freeman, and all the staff at Urbanworks. To Marshall Robinson, Beetlebome, and wife. To my uncles, aunts, cousins, and my people in Atlanta, Ga.

I'd like to acknowledge the Improvs and Funny Bones. Club work is tough, and you keep it enjoyable.

To Outkast, Ludacris, Ying Yang Twins, Lil Jon, Goodie Mob. Thanks, for your support in the DIRTY SOUTH.

I don't give shout-outs, but wanted to thank Tom Joyner, J. Anthony Brown, and the morning team.

To Bodon, in Chicago, for making me look like a Playa. To Chef Al at Chanterelles for giving me another reason to come home.

To the Boogie Man, Gina Holland, and all my people from BET, and to Russell Simmons for giving us Def Comedy Jam. To Dan Consiglio and all my people at Cramer Krasselt. To Philip Fogleman and all my people at Popeyes for letting me have some fun.

To all of the black comedy clubs, promoters, and fellow comedians out there who keep me in the game and allow me to have some fun. Special thanks to Club 559 and to the Blue Flame Lounge, Ice Cube, Matt Alvarez, and Steve Harvey.

To everyone I may not have mentioned by name but that I carry with me every day.

To my special someone, you know who you are. You are an inspiration and my true friend. I value all that you are and all that I am when I'm with you.

Above all, I thank God for the wisdom and guidance and for always reminding me that I am no different than anybody else, maybe a little funnier, but we are all the same.

To my mom, *Ruby*,
for birthing me and keeping me focused at ALL times;

my kids, *Antwon*, *Branten*, and *Sekeitha*,
you are my everything;

my uncle, *Paul Henson Jr.*, and Auntie *Grace*; Aunt *Ernestine*;

my manager, *Adam Williamson*;

and of course, to *all of you* out there
who make this so enjoyable.

Contents

Introduction

If you've already got this far, then you are reading a book, which puts me at a disadvantage. You're not out in the audience, where I'm used to seeing you. I can't snap on what you're wearing, or make eye contact with you, or hear your reactions to what I'm saying. But if you have seen me on stage, then you've heard me say that I don't tell jokes, I tell stories about my life, and the people I have met in my life. Well, damn, a book is a fine place to tell stories. And it gave me the chance to go looking through a lot of years to tell them. A lot of those stories are funny, some of them are sad, some of them just ask you to understand where I'm coming from. The main thing is that I could cover a lot more of my life in a book than I can on stage. First of all, you'll get to take your time with all sorts of things I might not have gotten around to talking about up to now. And second of all, I won't get sidetracked by somebody walking in late wearing a messed-up shirt.   **1**

Leave Him Alone, He's Creative

I'm from Atlanta, Georgia, and Atlanta will always be home. Some people can't wait to go somewhere else. And once they're there, they can't wait to leave their hometown behind. Not me. If I'm in L.A., and something crazy happens on the news, I check it out for a second and think, "Well, that's L.A." But if something crazy happens in Atlanta, I ramp up the volume on the remote going "Everybody quiet down, this is from back home!" It doesn't have to be something wacky on the news, either. Sometimes I'll forget to take those airline baggage tags off my luggage, and I'll go to use it again, and see that "ATL" abbreviation for Atlanta on the tag, and I start getting emotional. Hell, I can even get all misty-eyed watching the Weather Channel give the forecast for Georgia. Sometimes I'll wait for them to actually show footage of Atlanta on the Weather Channel, you know, when they send the cameras out to see folks walking around whatever city they're talk-ing about.

My friend was over one time in L.A., and we're just hanging out, and he realized I had been watching the Weather Channel and gone all quiet.

"Bruce," he said. "Are you crying, bro?"

"Shut up! I ain't crying!"

"Bruce, man, it's only a shot of people with umbrellas walking on Peachtree."

"I am not crying. Shut UP!"

Luckily, I'm able to get back to Atlanta pretty often. My mother is still there. My mother is my girl. But like a lot of folks from her generation, she doesn't understand what I do for a living. She doesn't think I do anything for a living. She didn't even believe I was the host of *Coming to the Stage*. She called me on the phone one day.

"Hey, Bruce?"

"Yes, Mama?"

"I'm looking at *Coming to the Stage*, and there's a guy on there that looks just like you."

"Mama, that *is* me."

"No. That can't be."

"It's me, Mama."

"No. This fella is *sharp as hell*."

That's my mother. She still hollers into the cell phone like you can't hear her otherwise. I have to tell her, "Hey, Mama, turn the volume on your mouth down to 2, 'cause it's at around 23 right now."

She raised me for most of my younger days at 415 Chestnut Street N.W., Apartment #8. My father left when I was still a little boy. But I was lucky, because at Chestnut Street, in an adjoining apartment, was my mother's sister's

4

husband, my uncle, Paul Henson Jr. He was like a father to me, no other way to say it. One of the greatest gifts my uncle gave to me was something he used to say all the time. He said it to folks who might wonder about me, about my being a little crazy or different. He used to say, *"Leave him alone, he's creative."*

See, I was an only child. I didn't have anyone before me to blaze the trail, and I didn't have anyone after me to set any kind of example for. I tried everything. I started small, by drawing all over the walls when I was real little. Mickey Mouse and Donald Duck and Fred Flintstone. First I drew them, then I got Magic Markers to color them in. Mom got bothered, but my uncle just said, "Leave him alone, he's creative."

I have a scar on my forehead you can still see if you're looking. I got that scar because when I was little I wanted to see what happened to a rock when it fell. I always carried a pocketful of rocks anyway, the flat, smooth kind because they were the best for flinging at your friends. So, I grabbed a handful of rocks and started tossing them in the air, one by one. Every time I threw one up, I'd lean my head back and watch that stone drop. Damn, I was really getting a great feeling for what happened to a rock when it fell! Then I threw one up, and it came back down on my head. Everybody said I was a damn fool. Not my uncle. He said, "Leave him alone, he's creative."

When I was around six or seven, I started wearing a whole bunch of stuff all at once. I don't know why, it just felt like the thing to do. I wore basketball pants with a football jersey, shoulder pads and a wrestling belt, a football helmet and cowboy boots. I got in the bathtub with my cowboy boots. I slept in those cowboy boots. By now, my uncle saying "Leave him alone, he's creative" had sunk in, I think, because people got awfully damn used to seeing me in six different kinds of clothing at one time.

Like any great world conqueror, I had to keep growing. I had to tap into new kinds of ambition. At ten, I rode my first roller coaster at Six Flags Over Georgia. I loved that roller coaster, and I figured every kid should have one of those in his backyard. So I built one. I went around the neighborhood collecting old broom handles. I must have gotten a hundred of them. I sawed the rounded ends off, then stuck them in the ground in a long, curvy line (since who the hell has ever heard of a straight roller coaster? Damn, I had a vision.). On top of the broomsticks I put flat pieces of board, which I used as the track. Now, what would I use to convey my roller coaster passengers on their terrifying ride of doom? I started with a Big Wheel, and that really was terrifying, since it only had three wheels. Many was the small child who fell headfirst onto the ground while we tried to keep the Big Wheel's one front tire on track.

"Bruce, this front wheel keeps wobbling."

"We'll just balance the back two. Go on."

"If you say *sooooooooooo*—!"

CRASH!

I will say this: it was a damn sight easier to be creative in the 1970s. Nowadays, someone would get their backside sued for the things we did when we were kids.

Anyway, we finally settled on a scooter to be our roller coaster vehicle. I painted it pink, and we put seven or eight little kids on it. We got some pretty good rides in, but they all ended the same way. With our butts taking a dirt bath.

Looking back, what I constructed was not really a roller coaster. More like a chunk of play area two feet off the damn ground. But to *us*, it was a roller coaster. To us, it was Six Flags Over Chestnut Street, dammit!

Come to think of it, if you were a little kid, which would you rather hear: "Cut that crap out" or "Leave him alone, he's creative"? It wasn't anything but a blessing. And it made me the tolerant man that I am today. For example, my mother's real name is Ruby, but she likes people to call her Carol. That's pretty messed up, but I leave her alone, because she's creative.

And now, after all these years of being left alone to be creative, my name is Bruce Bruce. You got that? Not Big Bruce. Not Fat Bruce. Not Big Fat Bruce. Not Big Fat Bruce Boy.

I was born Brantley Bruce Church. I'm proud of that name, proud of where I come from, but I became Bruce Bruce for you. I did. Don't lie now: if you're thinking you want to go out and see a comedian, is the name Brantley Bruce Church going to inspire a whole lot of confidence in you? Brantley Bruce Church will show you how to fix your damn computer. You're not going to hear the emcee holler, "Bring the love, for Brantley . . . Bruce . . . Churrrrrch!" I'm not saying there isn't room for a good Brantley Bruce Church in show business. If I had chosen a different path in entertainment, I might have kept my real name. I could have been the black guy on the soap opera, the one who talks like Don Cornelius, or Melvin Lindsey from *The Quiet Storm*, and always has his stereo system on in his apartment, so an alto saxophone solo can play softly behind him in every scene. The music always gets turned up when the loving starts, and then it's the same whether you're black or white. If you're on TV, and you're making love, you're doing it to saxophone music.

But I didn't want to be a soap opera star. I didn't even know I wanted to be a comedian. Since I can remember, all I knew was that people always said I was funny. In fact one of the preachers at my aunt Ernestine's church, who a lot of people in the congregation said was a prophet, once told me I would become a comedian. And that all started because ever since I was a little boy, I've been marking folks, observing them. And once I mark them, I imitate them.

Such as Mother Marshall, one of the regulars at Holiness Church. You could always tell when Mother Marsh was getting ready to testify, because her legs would start twitching, and that bottom of hers would start vibrating, getting ready to bounce up out of that pew. It was easy to make people laugh by imitating Mother Marsh going into spasms, or doing an impression of her husband, who would get up and move in little jerks, like a robot. I was already doing what I do now; not telling jokes, but using real life for laughs.

Years before Aunt Ernestine took me to Holiness Church, I'd have to put on my suit and tie and go to Greater Mountain Calvary Baptist Church with my mother and her sister Grace, Uncle Paul's wife. At Greater Mountain, everything was pretty orderly. The deacon said a prayer. The choir sang. There was an offering. The preacher preached the good word. And the deacon would come back and give the final benediction.

Sometimes my mother didn't have any money for the offering, so she would just touch the tray with her fingertips as it came by. Just a little pat on the edge of that tray, just enough to make it look like she may have dropped a little something in there. I'd see that tray coming by my face, and look over at Mama as it was going by hers.

She would say, "Praise God," and tap the tray.

I'd look over at her. "Mama, you didn't put no money in there."

And she would hiss at me in a whisper, "Shut your damn mouth!"

Cussing in church!

After church was when they all gathered outside and got right back into gossiping and talking trash, catching up on what was going on in everybody's life. Somebody always had a little baby, being showed around for the first time since it was born. The old ladies loved to go and look at the new babies.

"Look at that little one. Well, bless his heart."

That's what old people said when there was something wrong with somebody. "Bless his heart." If someone had an ugly baby, somebody else's grandma would always have something nice to say about it.

The grandma looks down at the tiny child. "Is that your baby?"

"Yes indeed."

"Really?" And the grandma gives a little pause before she pulls out the secret code phrase. "Well, bless his heart."

"Bless his heart" means that baby is *MESSED UP*!

Because come on, now, everybody's child is not cute. Somebody's got some real gorillas in the house. But like I said, at Greater Mountain Calvary Baptist Church, things were quiet and orderly.

Now, at Holiness Church, you had to testify. If you   **9**

had been helped by the Lord, then you had to stand up and say it!

"I just got a job. Thank you, God. Glorrrry!"

"If you're sitting here," the preacher would yell out, "then God has got you here! God woke you up this morning! Thank God for being woken up this morning!"

Ernestine would come home from work, make her dress, and wear it to church that night. Those dresses covered EVERYTHING! A woman couldn't show her neck, her arms, or her legs, and she had to have a head covering, and couldn't wear open-toed shoes. But just the same, you would think you were in a nightclub! The music was LOUUUDDD! They had a drummer, a bass player, a keyboard player, the whole deal. And you would sweat, man, would you sweat.

Ernestine would say, "Every time you stomp, you're kicking the devil in the head!"

At Holiness, people would get possessed by spirit and speak in tongues all the time. When I was a boy, I didn't understand what the hell was coming out of their mouths, but I would remember them by the English words they reminded me of. I can still hear those ladies, with their bodies shaking, and throwing their heads back, saying what sounded to me like:

"Saddam Hussein! Saddam Hussein!"

"Comin' in a Hyundai! Comin' in a Hyundai!"

"Untie my shoe, untie my shoe!" (This was a good one, because all of these ladies wore those big brown shoes that didn't have any laces.)

Then there was the woman named Damm who got up and said she just wanted to thank the Lord for her brother, her sister, her daughter, her husband . . . she just wanted to thank God for the whole Damm family! That's a true story. When you're in the heat of a testimony, you don't have time to think about how something is going to come out.

Kids and adults mixed a lot more back in the day. Their worlds intersected all the time. And adults knew this, because they had a whole set of grown-up ways to keep children out of their business. My mother would have people over, and one of them would say, "Hey, you want to hear a joke?"

And then everyone would realize that little Bruce was in the room, and they would all clear their throats and get these confused looks on their faces like they were all trying to hold in the same fart. How come everything stopped because of me?

Oh, I got it. That joke they were going to tell was a dirty one. Damn, it was probably one I'd already heard at school half a dozen times, and here they are thinking they have to protect me from such filth. Grown-ups don't know nothing about being little once they're big.

"Bruce," my mama would say, "I need you to find my brown belt for me."

"What you need your brown belt for right now?" I would ask, even though I knew why she wanted to get rid of me.

"Never mind, Bruce, I just need it. Now it's in my room somewhere, go and find it."

So off I'd go to her room, fishing around and finding nothing. Outside, suddenly everybody busted up laughing. When the laughter died down, my mother called out, "Did you find the belt, Bruce?"

And I would walk back out holding the only belt I could find, which was a black one.

"Oh, no, that's not my brown belt," she would say. "I don't know what I did with that brown belt of mine. Well, thank you for looking for it for me, baby."

"What should I do with this here belt, then?" I asked her.

"Just put it back, I guess."

"Mama?"

"Yes, Bruce?"

"You're wearing your brown belt right now, Mama."

"Oh, so I am. Well, never mind, Bruce. Be a good boy, now."

I played along. I knew that she knew why I was sent out of the room, and she knew that I knew why, too. Someone should tell grown-ups that they ought to just tell their kids to leave the room because they want to tell a dirty joke. Otherwise, a child could grow up with some *re-sentments* about having to go look for a damn *belt* in the middle of a dinner party.

Now, Aunt Grace, my uncle Paul's wife, she got the adult code-talking backward. A lot of times, when a grown-up doesn't want you to know what they are talking about, they spell the word instead of saying it. You know, like, "Is it okay for him to have a C-O-O-K-I-E?" or "Isn't it time for his N-A-P?" Grace came into my uncle's house when there was a surprise planned for me on my third birthday. Only she spelled the wrong word.

"Did you put the *toys* in the C-A-R?"

I sure didn't care about any car, but now I damn well knew where the toys were.

When they weren't speaking in code around you, adults were good at telling you what to do. And if you got sick as a child, the adults had their home cures, handed down through generations. Here was mine:

THE CHURCH FAMILY HOME MEDICAL ADVISOR

SYMPTOM	CURE
Chicken pox	Three swallows, Red Rock ginger ale
Hiccups	Nine glasses of water in a row without breathing
Common cold	A little honey, a little lemon, and a lot of cognac all mixed together. Draws that goddamn cold right out of you.
Stomachache	Castor oil
Cut knee	Castor oil
Earache	Castor oil
Bleeding profusely from open wound	Castor oil
Still losing blood, probably dying	Castor oil

There was a place for everybody while I was growing up. Even crazy people. They served a purpose in the neighborhood. You didn't need to pretend they weren't there.

Blan was the neighbor who lived catty-cornered to us. He was a college-educated man who worked at the post office. But on the weekends, he would get drunk, sit out on

his creaky old porch swing in nothing but his boxer drawers, and think he was a preacher. He would stand there
and shoot off his mouth for hours! But none of it was
about God, or religion, or being saved or anything. He
would just yell out a bunch of things that didn't make any
sense, but in the style of a preacher.

"Brothers and sisters! Treat yourself to a cool, refresh-
ing glass of lemonade today! For I say unto each of you,
The Atlanta Journal-Constitution is a fine publication! And,
brothers and sisters, how about this beautiful damn
weather?"

And as people passed he would greet them:

"Hello, young man! Bless you, dear heart! Lovely to
see you!"

Before long, everybody would sit on the porch across
the street and watch. Except Miss King, another neighbor,
who kept calling out, "Blan! Get back inside, you old
fool!"

Miss King would always get fed up and call the police,
and every time the police would come over and approach
Blan. But Blan was on his own property, on his own porch
swing, in nothing but a pair of boxer drawers.

Blan would say to the police, "I'm only giving the word
of God," and there wasn't much the police could do. He
wasn't really disturbing the peace, since everybody loved
to line up and watch him. He was really only disturbing
Miss King. And man, did he know that! He loved to rile
Miss King. After the police left, he would get up off the
porch swing and head back inside. Miss King would
breathe a sigh of relief, but we all knew what was coming.
He was just going inside to change into a new pair of
boxer drawers, the pair with a painting of lips on the

crotch side *and* the butt side. He'd wiggle them drawers at Miss King until she blushed and went back inside. I'll never forget Blan. Every neighborhood needs a Blan.

On weekends, there would be a bunch of guys singing doo-wop on the corner, and I'd ride my bicycle right down through the middle of them. They'd be singing some song, "I love you so-oh, wee-oooh," and there I came, barreling through and razzing them, singing something by Ray, Goodman & Brown just to throw them off their Moonglows rhythm. It worked even better if I could pedal that bike through a puddle at the same time.

"Damn you, Bruce!" they would yell, and one or two of them would chase after me until he got winded. It was a game, and we were both playing it. This was the neighborhood.

The McGintys were a family of fifteen boys. The only person who could handle them was their big, stocky, scary-ass mother. These boys were gentlemen, and hustlers, and they would not hesitate to kill a man if they figured it needed doing.

Every day during the summer one of those McGinty boys (Which one? Who the hell knows? There were fifteen of them!) would see me around the neighborhood, doing my stupid shit like setting a trash can on fire or whipping rocks at my friends, and dressing in basketball pants, football jersey, wrestling belt, shoulder pads, football helmet, and cowboy boots.

"You're crazy," that McGinty said to me.

I smiled and replied, "My uncle told me I was creative."

And that McGinty said, "No, Bruce. You're just crazy."

To hell with him. My uncle was right. **15**

Uncle Dad & the Milk and Fish Menace

No question, the most influential man in my life was my uncle, Paul Henson Jr. Four feet, nine inches tall with a sixty-inch waist, we called him Humpty Dumpty, but there was nothing but respect in it. He never raised a hand to me, never whooped me. He didn't have to. Just the thought of him getting mad enough to WANT to whoop me had me falling right into line. I loved him too much to even contemplate disappointing him. Stealing, lying, being selfish, these were all no-no's, and my uncle would kill me if I did any of them. And I didn't want to die.

My uncle taught me about respect ("When I tell you somethin', it's because I know what I'm talkin' about. If I don't know it, I won't say it"), he taught me how to treat women ("If you doin' the job right, you don't need more than one"), and he taught me how to cook. My uncle was a Gold Medal baking winner. Everybody wanted his cakes

BRUCE BRUCE

and pies and biscuits. When he bought a car, he didn't let the salesman say a word before he came in with "Lemme see the trunk." He needed a trunk big enough to hold all his baked goods. He always drove a Cadillac, nothing but a Cadillac. And he would never drive on the highway. NEVER. His job would call him:

"Paul, you need to deliver a cake. It's going to—"

"Hold on! You need to tell me the street way."

"The street way?"

"I ain't goin' on no highway. Those fools'll kill ya!"

Even on the "street way," my uncle was on the lookout for all the fools on the road just waiting to personally kill him. He'd mash his damn brakes and we'd all lurch forward in our seats going "What the hell?" And he would point out past the windshield at some car that was half a damn mile away!

"Did you see that son of a bitch?" he'd holler. "You see how he's driving? That fool'll get us all killed!"

"He's half a mile away!" I'd say to him.

"He ain't no half a mile away! He's a fool!"

The crazy thing is, I learned to drive in my uncle's car. Only he wasn't in it.

That 1968 Coupe de Ville looked mighty damn sweet to me and my grade-school friends. And every day after work, my uncle would take a good long nap, leaving the Caddy unattended. I was ten years old when I got the idea to take it for a ride while Uncle Paul was sleeping. I knew that my best buddy, Barry, would be down with this idea. We'd been in the same homeroom since first grade, and he would join in on everything I decided to try.

Barry would take a piece of chalk and mark the position of the Caddy's tires while it was parked, so we'd know

18

how to line it up when we came back. Then, I would get behind the wheel, and slowly back that mother out. I always felt that little *bump* of the right rear tire going onto the curb, then the *ca-thunk* of it dropping back down off the curb. I could barely see over the top of the steering wheel! When I got to the corner, everybody hopped in. Barry, our friend Rodney Turner, Yvette Lewis, my cousin Angela Church . . . ten kids! I put four girls in the front with me (you know it!). And five guys rode in the backseat.

That Cadillac went swerving all over Chestnut Street and beyond, with ten laughing, screaming ten-year-olds inside.

"Turn left, Bruce!"

"Shit!"

"That guy's trying to pass you!"

"You went up on the curb!"

"Red light!"

"Where's the damn brake?"

"Can't you reach the brake?"

"Hold on!"

"Agggghhhhh!"

This went on four or five times that summer, and we never once got stopped by the police. Maybe everybody just figured it was an old lady driving, and got out of the way. Turning around to go back was the scariest part. That big boat of an automobile must have looked like a giant metal version of a hopped-up Curly from *The Three Stooges*, spinning around and around in the middle of the street.

When we pulled back into the parking spot, Barry would guide me toward lining up the wheels onto exactly **19** where he'd made the chalk marks, and we were home free.

The day we quit was when we drove past the corner one day and heard some old guy say, "I just saw a ten-year-old driving a Cadillac!"

Never mind the police. If an old guy from the neighborhood said it, the whole damn town would know in an hour, and we'd be MESSED UP! But my uncle NEVER figured it out. One day I overheard him telling my aunt Grace about how he could swear there was less gas in his tank when he left than when he came home.

Damn, I'm glad I wasn't in the room when he said that, or I would have laughed and got caught, and he would have killed me. That was what I really loved about my uncle: I never doubted for one second that he would kill me, even though I knew he wouldn't kill me. You get it?

My uncle used reverse psychology to trick me into seeing how wrongheaded I was. When I was eight years old, I was curious about smoking. My uncle did not drink or smoke at all, but the next day he bought a pack of White Owls, and had me try one. I felt sick.

"You see how these things make you feel?" he said to me.

Later, I was curious about liquor. He let me have a big gulp of gin, and I couldn't stand it. It burned my throat!

"Now you see what I'm talkin' about?"

I still wanted to test those limits, though, so I went and had some beer. I got drunk, felt even sicker. My uncle told me what he was doing all along. "I'm breaking you of these habits," he told me. "They ain't going to do you no good, ever."

In third grade, they tested my eyes at school and told

me I was going to have to wear glasses. This was a major trauma in third grade. They might as well have said they could already tell I was homosexual.

My uncle said, "You don't want to wear those glasses, Bruce, is that right?"

"No way!" I said. "I'm not wearing glasses! A lot of sissies and nerds wear 'em. I'm not wearing no damn glasses!"

"Is that so?"

"That's so!"

"Well," he said, "I remember when they told me to wear glasses. I refused to do it, just like you."

"That's good," I said.

"They told me if I wore them for just a little while, it would probably see me through for a time, and after that I may never need them again. I told them they were six kinds of fool if they thought they could say anything to make me wear a pair of glasses."

"Right on. You right," I told him.

"Close your eyes," my uncle said.

"What?"

"Just close your damn eyes like I tell you."

I did.

"Now, what do you see?" he asked me.

"I don't see nothin'."

"That's exactly what you're gonna see if you don't wear them glasses."

I opened my eyes, and my uncle held a pair of glasses in his palm. The ones he had to use now. He didn't need to say anything else. I wore glasses for a year, and then my eyes got better, and I never had to wear them again. I put up with some shit, but once again, my uncle taught me **21** how to get through it. Sure, he was messing with my head, but when you're at a young age, you're asking to have your head messed with. You *want* some damn direction!

If something stupid I did was ever threatening to get my uncle out of his chair, he would say, "If I have to get up from this table, I'm gonna shoot everybody, and then give 'em a good talkin' to."

My uncle loved Westerns.

"Clint Eastwood comin' on tonight!" he'd call out, and I'd go put on my cowboy boots and toy gun belt. We'd watch the shoot-'em-up on TV, but my uncle would watch me playing with my toy guns, and he would take the time to explain that what I was watching was just an act. He was letting me know when to draw the line between reality and fantasy.

"But you always say you're gonna shoot everybody," I said.

"I'm just talkin'," he said. And when we watched Clint Eastwood together, every commercial break, he would make sure I heard him when he said, "Remember, Bruce, you don't go around killin' people." That's some damn good advice, don't you think?

My uncle always made sure I knew what a real man was. It didn't have anything to do with guns or drinking or drugs. It had to do with honesty, integrity, and the way you treat other people, especially women.

"A real man makes sure he keeps it real, and he makes sure the woman keeps it real, too. It's about having responsibility, and feeding your kids. A man who doesn't feed his kids is not a real man."

To this day, I leave big tips in restaurants, because I can still remember going to the Varsity in Atlanta for hamburgers with my uncle. He would drive us into the parking lot for the curbside service, and I would see the servers fighting over who got to go to his car.

"I got him!"

"Shut up! You had him last time!"

"How come they all want to come to your car?" I asked my uncle.

"Because I tip good. I take care of them."

And since then, I have worked in the restaurant business. So, the big tipping thing is not about showing off, or letting people know I'm a player. It's about letting people know they are appreciated. I know that every person taking care of my needs in a restaurant or a club has a family, or school to pay for, or bills to get to. I may not have developed an understanding of community like that if not for my uncle.

My uncle taught me that a parent can be quick to tell a child when they've done something wrong, but then forget to tell them when they've done something good. I surely remember my uncle saying two things to me on a regular basis.

1. "Bruce . . . that was *real* dumb."

2. "Now that's what I'm talkin' about, Bruce!"

There is no substitute for having someone in your life who wants to see you go further. And someone who accepts you for who you are. Even when you're a dumb-ass little third grade boy who believes everything his dumb-ass friends tell him.

You know how when you're little, and your friends **23**

start talking about these nasty things they heard about, and pretty soon they're totally true, because you heard it from your friend who heard it from his sister, who knew somebody who worked at the hospital, and they were there when they brought in the dead guy? In third grade, this stuff is SCARY. There was the one about that bug that could crawl into your ear and eat all the way through your brain and come out the other ear. That's some freaky shit. Or the alligator that came right up through that man's toilet and bit him something painful while he was going number two. For real! The alligator escaped from the zoo and got into the sewer system, and crawled all through the pipes into this guy's house!

So, knowing how susceptible us little kids were to these stories, it's no surprise that for a full six months, the talk going around English Avenue Elementary School was that eating milk and fish together can kill you. I don't think that rumor got circulated anywhere but at my school. I'm sure you all have your stories from when you were little bitty kids, but don't even try to tell me you knew about the fish-and-milk-together-can-kill-you one, because this one was ours. And we believed it, let me tell you! Ain't nobody we knew was gonna be fool enough to eat milk and fish!

"Oh, yeah! You didn't hear about that guy? Took a bite out of his catfish, reached for that glass of milk, gulped it down, and WHAM! Killed him dead!"

You should have seen us in the lunch line, creeping along with our trays, eyes wide open, sticking our necks out to see if they were giving us fish that day. Fish days were the worst. You'd be shaking so hard your Jell-O dessert would be wiggling all the way to the lady at the end. Then she tries to give you your little carton of milk to go with it, and you're jerking your little head back and forth with your lips all shut tight, saying, "Nnh-nnh."

And the lunch lady says, "What's the matter with you? You got to drink your milk with your lunch!"

And we're going, "Nnh-nnh."

And she gets all mad and makes us take the milk anyway, and she's looking over her shoulder and watching us the whole time we're eating, wondering why we're so scared of a little damn milk. So we open the carton, making sure she can see us pushing back the flaps, and after we take a bite of the fish we pretend to drink the milk, bringing it up to our lips and tilting our heads back, all the while smiling and looking over at the lunch lady so she thinks we're drinking it for real. One time my friend Rodney thought he touched a little bit of the milk when he was fake-drinking it. That boy froze up like he'd just seen a ghost.

"Whaaat? Are you sure, Rodney? You drank some milk?"

"I'm pretty sure."

"After you already started eating your fish?"

"Yeah."

"Ohhhhhh . . ."

"Watch him . . . he's going to die."

"You think I'm going to die?"

"You said you drank some milk!"

"I don't know. It felt like I touched a little milk."

"Shit. Do you feel like you're dying?"

"Maybe. A little."

"What's it feel like?

"Like I'm dying."

"Yeah, but what's that feel like?"

"Like I can't breathe."

"But you can breathe, right? You're breathing now, right?"

"Yeah, but it feels like I can't."

"How can it feel like you can't breathe if you're breathing?"

"I don't know!"

"Wait. I think he's okay."

"Maybe it was just that moisture, you know, the wet drops that build up on the carton while it's up there in the lunch line. Maybe that's all you touched with your lips."

"Oh, man, you think that could be it?"

"Yeah. I don't think any milk got onto you."

We all took our cartons of milk and threw them out when the lunch lady went out to use the bathroom. We were terrified of that milk and fish shit.

One day, I was over at my uncle Paul's, and he was having fish for dinner. But not just fish. He poured himself a glass of milk.

"No!" I reached out to stop him grabbing the glass. I didn't want my uncle to die!

"What's the matter with you, Bruce?"

"Don't drink the milk. Fish and milk will kill you!"

"What in the hell are you talking about? Fish and milk can't kill you!"

"Yes it can!"

He took a bite of fish. I started to sweat. He went for the milk. I reached out to stop him again.

"Bruce! Don't make me shoot you!" Then he drank that milk down, took a big gulp. I put my hands in front of my face. I couldn't look.

"Open your eyes, Bruce," my uncle said. "Do I look dead to you?"

He sure didn't, but that wasn't enough for me. Maybe the milk and fish combo crept up on you, like a slow-acting poison from the movies.

"You're getting ready to die, then!" I said, all high-pitched in my scared-little-boy voice.

"Nobody's getting ready to die. Now shut your mouth."

So I shut up, but all night long I watched him. He seemed to be moving around like normal. He watched all of *Gunsmoke* without kicking the bucket. He got himself ready for bed without keeling over on me.

But I still wasn't convinced.

While he was sleeping, I snuck into his room and watched him. You don't spend half a year hearing about how milk and fish can kill you and not need to be completely damn sure! At least not in third grade. I stared at my uncle all night, making sure his shoulders were rising up and down, making sure he was still breathing. A couple of times he snored, and these weren't just snores. Just like, when he was awake, his coughs weren't just coughs. When my uncle coughed, it sounded like he was trying to get every single drop of wet shit that was ever in his lungs out in one big blast. And when he snored, man, the air in his nostrils snapped, crackled, and popped like a million Rice Krispies going off one at a time underwater. This is a scary sound to a kid who's been up all night keeping a vigil next to his uncle's bed to make sure that he isn't going to die from milk-and-fish disease. So when he would snore, I'd get all panicky, and poke him until he woke up.

27

"What the hell are you doing here, you damn fool?" my uncle said.

"I thought you were choking!" I told him. "From the milk and fish!"

"You woke me up about milk and fish again?"

"You sounded like you were dying!"

"Damn it, I ain't dead, Bruce. Now, will you shut up about milk and fish and get your paranoid ass to bed!"

I finally did go to sleep, and I was real glad to see my uncle still alive the next morning. But to this day, I don't mess with milk and fish.

James Brown

When you're good at marking people and imitating them, you're in demand. People will say, "Bruce, do Mother Marshall!" Or, "Bruce, do your granddaddy when he gets mad, you know the way he leans back with his belly all hangin' out!" And my talent for marking folks was not limited to neighborhood folks. One weekend, when I was seven or eight years old, I was sound asleep when my mother came into the room.

"Bruce, wake up."

"What? Huh? Is that you, Mama?"

It was three o'clock in the morning. She started slapping me on the face.

"Come on, Bruce, wake up!"

"What you want, Mama?"

"Do James Brown."

"What?"

"Come on out and do James Brown for everybody."

Well, I guess my mama had some people over that Friday night, and they all got to talking and drinking and carrying on, and it came up that I could impersonate James Brown.

"Mama, I'm tired."

"You always want people to pay attention to you, Bruce. You're always doing some fool thing to get a rise out of folks, and now you have the chance to impress a whole room full of my guests, and you're saying no?"

Damn. She had me there. But I was going to play out the power struggle a few seconds longer. I got all diva on her. "I can't just get out of bed and do James Brown, Mama!"

"The hell you can't! Now I went and told everyone that your James Brown is something to see. Are you gonna let your mama look like a liar in front of all them people?"

The power struggle was officially over. "I guess not, Mama."

"Now you're talkin'. Come on, now."

I went out to the front room, still pretty groggy. My audience was about four or five of my mother's friends, neighbors, people she knew from H.L. Greene, the department store where she worked. It's remarkable how just a few people talking all at once can seem so loud, especially at three o'clock in the morning. But every one of their voices stopped dead when they turned around to see me coming in. Then, I stared back at them. I sure as hell wasn't going to just launch into James Brown on my own.

There was a few seconds of awkward silence, which got broken by Mama.

"Go on, Bruce. Do your James Brown."

There they were. All these half-in-the-bag grown-up faces grinning at me, waiting for the show. I looked from one face to the other, each one of them with this wide-eyed expression of expectation. Mama had prepared them for something magical. I couldn't afford to let them down.

I realized I hadn't said a word, and I couldn't think of anything to say anyway. The whole thing felt kind of weird, so the only thing to do was to do it. In a split second, I allowed myself to become possessed by the spirit of the Godfather of Soul.

"Hgnh!" I did the James Brown grunt, and started to shuffle my feet and shimmy around, getting on my good foot. The grown-ups started hollering right away. They were shifting their own hips around from where they sat, jabbing out their arms, urging me on. They didn't seem to mind that an eight-year-old was singing "Sex Machine."

"Get up, get on up . . . get up, get on up . . . stay on the scene, like a sex machine! Hgnh!" And then, the moment they had all been waiting for. I did the split! My legs flew out in opposite directions and hit the ground perfectly.

"Whooooo!" the call went up. I decided to leave on a high note, so I gave one final "Hgnh!" and stopped. Mama came up and put her arms around me.

"Didn't I tell you?" she was saying to everyone. "Damn!"

Just as suddenly as I'd popped into becoming James Brown, I popped back into a sleepy little boy.

"Can I go back to bed now, Mama?"

"Go on, then," she said.

And that was that. I can still remember the sound of jumbled-up adult voices remarking on my performance as I went back into my room and closed the door.

"That boy is something."

"Funny!"

"He's got talent, you know that, don't you?"

I was too small to think about what all that approval meant, but I knew I liked it, and that I had made my mama happy. Not too long after that, I would be very glad she got me up at three in the morning, because it let me do a kind of dry run of the act, getting me ready for the day when it would really count.

I don't remember what James Brown was doing at Six Flags Over Georgia in the mid-1960s, but there he was, right in the middle of the park.

"Mama, that's James Brown!" All I could do was stare at him. I just kept staring. If I didn't act fast, he would get away.

Mama nudged me. "Go and talk to him, Bruce!"

So I did.

"Mr. Brown!"

"Yes, sir," said the Godfather of Soul. "What's your name, son?"

"I'm Bruce, and I can dance just like you!"

"Is that so? I'd like to see that."

And I gave it all I had. Man, I moved like I had no bones. I danced like a three-foot-high Papa with a brand-new bag. I even did a "Hgnh!" I couldn't help myself. And then I brought it on home, with the big finish . . . the split!

James Brown himself flashed me that big Cheshire cat grin of his. "That was something else, young man! Gimme five, Bruce!"

What the hell else do you do when James Brown asks you to give him five? I gave him five.

"Now," he went on, "gimme some skin on the sideways!"

I gave him some skin on the sideways, you bet your ass I did. Then he walked off with his handlers. I watched him as he got smaller, got swallowed up by the crowd in the park. The whole thing was over in twenty seconds, which was probably a lot for a man like James Brown to spare on any given day. I was too little to think about it then, but now I suppose that's as good a description as any of being a celebrity. Aside from a few close friends, most of the people you meet get about twenty seconds.

School Days

I was a devilish boy, the kind who couldn't stop making myself a nuisance. The kind who was always up to something, but nothing too serious. In other words, I wouldn't ruin your life, but I'd annoy the hell out of you. Like the rocks I kept in my pocket, in case I needed to pop somebody on short notice. I carried a slingshot, too, and I was always threatening to shoot everybody with it. I think I picked up the idea of shooting everybody from my uncle. I never carried out the threat any more than he did.

I'd call up my cousin just to say, "We're gonna beat your ass in football tomorrow," and then when my team lost, I'd throw out some stuff like, "Man, too bad our key player got sick and couldn't play, or we would've beat your butt, sucker!"

And I could dance around the truth just enough so I didn't have to lie.

"Who set the trash can on fire, Bruce?"

"I seen that."

"Yes, but did you set the trash can on fire, Bruce?"

"The trash can got set on fire. Man, it was something."

"Who did it, Bruce?"

"I saw somebody do it." Damn, I loved that one. It was psychologically deep, you know? Because yeah, I saw somebody do it—it was me. But this was saying that without saying it. That is some award-winning Eddie Haskell jive, brother.

I picked on Vonda Freeman a lot. My favorite thing to do with Vonda was sneak something out of her pocketbook without her knowing. Vonda was the girl who always raised her hand to answer everything. Of course, back then I didn't know I was just jealous of her for knowing more than me, all I knew was that no one was supposed to be too smart when you're in elementary school. Vonda sat in front of me in Miss Powell's fifth-grade class, and when she wasn't raising her smart-aleck hand she was brushing her stupid hair. I got so tired of watching that brush get dragged through that rat's nest of hers that I reached over and took her comb and brush out of her pocketbook. Miss Powell saw the whole thing. She called me after class.

"Bruce, are you going to be a fool your whole life?"

I thought for a minute, then answered her with a straight face. "You know what, Miss Powell? I think I am."

I guess my overall memory of my grade-school years was that if something stupid happened, I was in the middle of it. Mr. Hammond, the principal, he could never witness me in the act of doing anything, which only made him want to get me all the more. My favorite catch-me-if-you-can game was to keep on shooting hoops after the break bell rang and we were supposed to go back inside. I'd make my buddy Jerry stay out there and shoot with me.

"Bruce, man, didn't you hear the bell? Hammond's watching through the window, you know he is."

Mr. Hammond did watch through the window, and I knew it, so I would bounce that ball as hard and loud as I could. Then, just when I saw movement inside his office, I would bolt off, too fast for him to get a look at me. But poor Jerry could never get the timing down like I did, and one time Hammond snagged him. That meant it was time for the "boom-boom pad." I was fortunate enough never to have been on the receiving end of the boom-boom pad, but Jerry told me about it after he got caught on the basketball court.

"He made me lean over the desk, and then he whacked my ass with that boom-boom pad."

"What's it look like?"

"It's like a big old piece of wood with, like, a piece of plastic or foam or something nailed to one side. Looks like he cut a piece out of a seat in the gym and stuck it on there."

"How many times he whack you?"

"Three. That thing hurts like hell."

"What the hell'd you say?"

"I said, 'Owwwwwwwwww!'"

Oddly enough, my first encounter with Mr. Hammond was under much different circumstances. It was in third grade, before I had truly discovered my potential for mischief. I wanted power and I figured I could get it as a Patrol Boy. A Patrol Boy's job was to make sure everybody filed into school when the bell rang, and to enforce the

"No running in the halls" rule. You got to wear an orange shoulder strap with a badge pinned to it, and if you saw anybody straggling and running, you could chew their ass out. This job was tailor-made for me. But if I wanted it, I had to interview for it. And I had to be interviewed by Mr. Hammond.

I was terrified to go into that office. First of all, Mr. Hammond wore Hai Karate cologne, and you could smell that shit from two hallways away. I remember the scent of Hai Karate getting stronger and stronger as I got closer and closer to the principal's office and knocked on the door.

"Come in. Oh, hello, Bruce. Miss Johnson tells me you're interested in being a Patrol Boy."

Patrol Boy? Man, if I had thought about how nerdy that job title sounded, I would have reconsidered. Instead, I said, "Yeah."

"It's 'Yes, sir!' And stand at attention when you're spoken to!"

Damn. This man was straight-up scary. "Yes, sir," I squeaked.

"Now, Bruce, do you think you can handle this job?

"Yes, sir."

"That orange strap and that Patrol Boy badge carry with them a great deal of respect in this institution. Are you prepared to uphold that trust?"

I had no idea what the hell he was talking about, but I figured it was good for another "Yes, sir."

"All right then." And he handed me the orange strap with the badge on it, and told me to report for training starting tomorrow. Then, he warned me that he arrived at school promptly at ten minutes to eight each morning, and that he would be looking for me as I helped the students file in by eight o'clock. "And if I should drive by and see that you are not there, that you are not doing your job, there will be a problem, do you understand, Bruce?"

"Yes, sir." What else was I going to say?

I'm proud to say that I performed my duties admirably, and retired my Patrol Boy strap and badge three months later. I'm sure I was motivated mostly by my fear of Mr. Hammond. And I think it was that fear of him that added the extra thrill as I got older and kept flying under his Hai Karate radar.

Like what happened in fifth grade, the year I met a girl with the tiniest ponytail you have ever seen in your whole life. Her name was Sharon Scott, and I don't know how she got her hair tied back so tight. There was just this little bitty piece of hair sticking out in back that you could barely see. It wouldn't even fit between your fingers. It was like when you blew up a balloon; that little tied-off bit at the bottom, that's how tight this ponytail was. Now, any man knows that when you are a boy, you already think you're a Mack Daddy, except you think the way to a girl's heart is to tease her. This is our way of not dealing with the fact that we like girls. A good insult is a form of affection from a young player. I only wish the girls in my school understood that. Damn, but I liked to make fun of Sharon's ponytail.

"Girl, how'd you get that teensy little ponytail, anyway?"

"What are you talkin' about?"

"Look at that thing! How'd you get that thing tied? I'll bet your mama had to put a foot in your back, your brothers had to yank back on your arms, and your sister had to stretch your neck back while your cousin pulled on your **41** hair and your other sister snapped that rubber band down on that pea-sized bit of hair that was left over." Seriously, man, I couldn't think of any other way this ponytail could have come to be.

Sharon stared at me for a while. I could tell she was thinking long and hard about how to respond to me. "I'm gonna beat your ass after school," she said. She was dead serious.

Three o'clock came around, and I stepped outside and saw Sharon waiting for me. Her friends were backing her up. My friends were backing me up. The only thing I could do was wait until school got out, and accept my punishment like a mature young man.

I ran my ass off.

I got a good lead, but Sharon shot after me like a track star. Damn, that girl could run. My boys are cheering me on, "Go, Bruce, go!" but the whole time they can see that Sharon is gaining on me. Now I start laughing. I'm running as fast as I can, and laughing. You know this pissed off Sharon even more. Suddenly, the voices of my friends stopped yelling out, and I knew Sharon was right behind me, ready to beat my ass just like she'd promised! She brought me down in a tackle, real hard. She put her knee in my back, and my face in a headlock.

"Whose ponytail is short now, huh?" She twisted my neck and ground that knee deeper into my back.

"It's still short!" I screamed back at her.

"What'd you say?"

"I said it's still short!"

"Urrggh!" she grunted like a linebacker, sinking the knee deeper, daring me to give in. "Take it back!"

42   "No!"

"Take it back!"

"I won't!"

"Take it back!"

The only thing to do here was a complete changeup. "I love you!"

That did the trick. She suddenly stopped jerking my head around. The pressure on my back from her knee eased up. "What?" she asked.

"I think I love you, Sharon!"

Now she stepped off me altogether. Her girls and my boys were standing around us, wondering what would happen next.

"You're crazy!" she said. She walked off. I picked the dirt out of my teeth and held my head up high. Another victory for Bruce, the Mack Daddy of the fifth grade, the doctor of love. Doctor of trash-talking more like. I was so scared of girls. I pulled their hair, knocked down their books just to get their attention and try out my lines. There was a girl called Portia who got all my best ones.

"I'm gonna be your man, real soon. . . ." ". . . That's right. Any day now, you'll be calling me sugar daddy . . ." ". . . You hear that Stylistics song, baby? That's me singing that, baby."

Truth is, if Portia would have said, "Come on, let's go," I would have frozen in place like a wigged-out Barney Fife. And not just in the fifth grade.

It was senior year of high school when Portia finally called me on my rap.

"Bruce, you've been talking all this trash for years. Well, my mom and dad and sisters are all out of town. Meet me behind the gym at three o'clock, and we'll head on over to my house."

Oh, yeah! That's more like it! The last time a girl had told me to meet her at three o'clock, it was Sharon Scott, and that was so she could beat my ass. This was different. This was Portia. Man, was I . . .

Afraid. Shit scared.

My friend Macheto drove me to the meeting place early. He parked a good ways away so we could watch for Portia without her knowing I was there. We sat there waiting in my 1974 Caprice Classic with tinted windows. Thank you, Jesus, for those tinted windows. When three o'clock came around, we saw Portia show up at the gym, walk around back, and then start to pace around. I laid down in the backseat of the car hiding, watching her slowly realize that Bruce wasn't going to be showing up.

Me and Macheto waited there until Portia finally got fed up and left. Then, we drove away and hooked up with another one of our buddies for the afternoon.

I'm not sure where the fear came from that day, but I'll bet my uncle had something to do with it. My uncle was not comfortable being a player. "For one thing," he used to tell me, "it costs a lot of money. Plus, I'm not a good liar." Here is a short list of my uncle's advice to me on the birds and the bees:

When I was twelve, the hard-line:

"If I catch you doing the nasty, I'm gonna kill everybody in the house." I didn't want anybody killed, so I didn't do the nasty.

When I was sixteen, sensitivity training:

"What girl do you like?"

"Jill Griel."

"Have you ever done the nasty?"

"She won't let me."

"Well, good for her. And you can't just go and take it, either!"

When I was eighteen, man-to-man practical advice:

"Put a helmet on your soldier."

One thing was for sure, as the years went by, I realized that pulling on Vonda Freeman's hair and stealing her brush was not going to cut it. Plus, by the time I got to high school, I saw that more and more women liked smart guys. Now, men, you may not have believed it back when you were in your teens, but that was the secret they didn't show you on TV. Girls like them smart.

Now, you're always going to get a percentage of fool women who are attracted to fool men, but the really valuable females are looking for brains. The trick for me was to find that delicate balance between smart and *cool*. If you were *only* smart, then you were a nerd, and even though you would eventually get your revenge by running the whole damn corporation that pays out minimum wage to all the guys who picked on you at school, that was years off, and you sure weren't going to get any booty in high school as a nerd.

Now, I wasn't smart in the conventional way, but I was sharp. So my strategy to impress girls in class was to answer as many questions as I could, even though I got a huge percentage of them wrong.

"Absolutely . . . positively . . . wrong," as Mr. Bell used to say. Mr. Bell taught U.S. Law, and he would go over the day's newspaper every day in class. He really wanted us to be up on current events, but unfortunately we didn't give a damn. I wish I could remember the name of the boy who raised his hand to answer Mr. Bell's question about the hostage crisis in Iran in 1979. None of us really knew **45** about the politics behind the whole thing, but one brave young man put out a theory. Brother, if you're out there reading this, know that you really made an impression on me with the sheer cajones it took to tell Mr. Bell the way you figured it went down.

"Um . . . the U.S. Army went to rescue the hostages, but they didn't know how hot it was in Iran, and the heat was too much for their helicopters, so they could have surprised the Iranians, but when the helicopters started breaking down and crashing, then the Iranians figured out they were there."

After that, no one attempted to fake their way through an answer again. There was just no topping it. So from then on, when Bell called on me, I had a standard response ready. "Mr. Bell, I am not adequately prepared to answer that question." Luckily, he never asked me when I thought I would be adequately prepared.

Then there was Mr. Lawson, who taught a class that to this day I could not tell you what it was about. Did you ever have a class like that, like "What the hell is he even saying?" I don't even remember what it was called, or what he was supposed to be teaching us when he got up there in front of the class. Mr. Lawson wore three different shades of black every day. What I remember most about him, and why I remember his class at all, is that he would make up words, English words that didn't exist.

"That was very latistic, Bruce." I knew there was no word "latistic," but this guy had definitions for his fake words, too. "It means your answer shows that you are very artistic, but a little lazy."

Damn. He was right. Like my uncle said: "Leave him alone, he's creative."

46

Baby James Brown

My homeroom teacher Miss Flagg retired when I was in tenth grade, and we got Mr. Ward for the remainder of my high school years. He got so furious with me for all of my clowning, but he never chose to discipline me. I got the feeling he felt like he should, but then he would laugh along with me as often as he'd get pissed off. Toward the end of high school, he said to me, "Bruce, you need to do something with that talent you got, because you are extremely funny." It would be years before I would follow his advice, but I will not soon forget the day I saw him out there in the audience of one of my shows. He came and saw me afterward, and shook my hand. I was smiling real big; it was good to see him again.

He said to me, "I knew you were going to be a comedian."

There was more communication between adults and kids back then, more of an understanding of how valuable it was to learn things. You learned from your teachers *talking*, which made you want to *listen*.

By my sophomore, junior, and senior years in high school, there was only one thing in my life that took more of my time than women, and that was the ROTC. It was my last class on Mondays, and I loved coming to school wearing that uniform, ready for the end of the day. The ROTC officer would check the creases on my pants. This was serious stuff, and man, I took it seriously. I was second in command. My buddy Macheto, the one who helped me hide from Portia, he was the battalion commander. And our favorite thing of all was drill team. Marching in precision, turning those rifles over. We were great at it.

One of our buddies on drill team was Terence Todd. **47**

He was cockeyed; one eye going off to the side. He couldn't see right, so he'd always drop the rifle. One day, our whole unit was marching in drill formation. Twenty-four guys, four lines, six guys in each line. Beside us were the flag girls—flag girls, who marched with us and carried the American flag, flipping it around just like we were flipping our rifles. I'm the leader of the front line, and I cannot mess up, you understand? Well, as we go marching past one of the flag girls, this guy from the second line, Kenny Arnold, grabbed the booty of one of the flag girls. I laughed when I saw it happen, and damned if that flag girl doesn't think it was me who grabbed her behind! So, she did what any young woman would do to express her discontent with such behavior: she kicked me in the damn nuts! Everything in front of my face went dark, and I grabbed onto my rifle to steady myself as I went down to the ground.

Stuart Johnson was a senior and captain of the drill team. He stood over me while my entire crotch was burning in pain, and I tried like hell to stand by bracing myself against my rifle.

"Get your sorry ass up!" says Stuart. I can still feel how badly those words stung, because it *wasn't me* who had started the whole thing! But there was no use telling him, I'd only look more like a fool. And then, I was saved at the last minute, by—guess who—Terence Todd!

"It was Kenny Arnold," Terence told Stuart. "He did it."

Thank you, Jesus! Terence had seen the whole thing out the corner of his beautiful lazy eye!

Well, I figured that flag girl owed me an apology, but you know, she never did give me one. She just looked at Stuart Johnson, and then back at me, and said, "That's what he gets for laughing." That is messed up! I don't know where that flag girl is now, but I'll bet her man doesn't laugh too much.

Damn, though, I loved drill team. The best thing about it, the thing I loved most, was when we were through for the day, and we marched back to that ROTC house in perfect cadence. It was really beautiful. And I needed some order in my life, because sometimes things got a little crazy, even for me.

Mama and Me

My mother and father divorced when I was six, and when my mama started dating I didn't like any other man but my father. You know how little kids are. When I was six, I already knew some good cuss words and everything. So Mama would have a boyfriend every once in a while that would come over and try to get on *her* good side by getting on *my* good side. Well, I didn't play. I didn't like this man, he wasn't my daddy. But he'd come over after church every Sunday and Mama would be in the kitchen getting some cookies and coffee for him or something, and the two of us would be left alone in the other room. He would sit there, looking at some cartoon I was watching on TV. I'm sitting there, and I don't like him, so when he looks over at me, I glare at him and I say, "What you looking at, you *ugly old dog*?"

He'd call my mama into the room and say, "Look here,

this boy thinks he can talk to me any old way, and I ain't gonna put up with this."

But I was slick. I'd look like a little angel and say, "Mama, I ain't said nothin' to him. I like him."

She'd say, "All right now, Bruce, you be good."

I'd say, "Yes, ma'am."

Then, my mother would walk back into the kitchen, and I'd look back at the man, with my little-boy chin all pushed up into my lower lip.

I'd say, "Oh, so you went and told on me, *you old bastard.*"

He'd say, "You're a bastard!"

"You are! You're the bastard. You can't even . . ." My six-year-old brain is trying real hard to come up with something nasty. "You can't . . . even . . . do . . . nothin'." I know it's not that good, so I say it again, meaner. "You can't . . . even . . . do . . . nothin'!"

But I got him going. I got a grown man to argue with a little kid. I won.

For a while, anyway.

I was eight years old when my mom's first real serious boyfriend first showed up. Our furnace went out, and this man came to fix the heater. Then he came to fix the heater the day after that. And the day after that. I didn't like him. I went to my uncle and I said, "There's a guy coming to fix the heater every single day!" At that time, Uncle Paul lived in an adjoining apartment to ours.

He went to talk to my mother. "What's this I hear about a man coming to fix your furnace five days running?"

"Who told you that?" she said.

"Never mind," said my uncle. "Tell him to fix the damn thing and get the hell home. Bruce don't like him."

It didn't matter to my mother, or maybe she just never understood why I didn't like the man. God bless my mom, she likes what she likes, that's what I always said about her. She was naive, too, because somewhere inside she knew this man was no good, and she still called him her boyfriend for ten full years, all the way through my schooling.

And I would see this SOB around town, too, with other women! That was how he played, you see, calling on women home alone during the day to fix their air conditioner or refrigerator. One day, I'm out driving with my boys, and we stop at a light. I'm sitting in the rear passenger side (that was my seat; always rear passenger side), and I look out the window and there's my mom's boyfriend with another woman sitting right next to him! That's messed up! He turned and saw me, too, staring at him hard. I looked him right in the eye, sending him that message: "I see you, right?" He didn't say nothing, just drove away.

What I didn't like about this man was that, even though he was a player and wasn't my real father, and wasn't even around all that much, he always tried to run things when he *was* around. By the time I got to be about thirteen, I was making it known that I did not approve of him. And he'd cuss me out when mom went into another room. He'd slap me around, too, tell me to clean up my room. I don't know how I put up with it as long as I did. Probably I was sparing my mother's feelings. But then I turned eighteen, and something snapped.

Back in the day, I was finishing up three years of ROTC, I was lifting weights, I was fit. I was a strong boy. It was the day of my baccalaureate, and in just a few minutes Macheto was going to pick me up in the famous 1974 Caprice Classic with tinted windows. This was my day. I'd worked hard, and I was proud of who I was. This was not the day for anyone to mess with me. But my mom's boyfriend wouldn't have cared if I was heading off to accept the damn Nobel Peace Prize, he'd still have some reason for getting up in my face. And that's what he did.

"Clean up this room," he said. Not very original. It was the same lazy-ass, this-is-what-a-male-authority-figure-is-supposed-to-say bull.

"Watch that, asshole," I said to him. "I ain't thirteen no more."

"Are you gonna clean up this room, or am I gonna beat you?"

He'd crossed the line for the last time. "My room is already clean," I said to him, "and why don't you try that beating. Go ahead."

The boyfriend made a big damn show of reaching down to pull his T-shirt off, like he was going to transform into Ali or something once he was bare-chested. Well, I made a show of something, too, and it stopped him in his tracks. I closed the door. Without a word being spoken, he knew what I was saying, and that was, *"Mom won't be walking in here to break this up. This is between us."* When I turned around, his arms were up over his head, as he finished removing the T-shirt.

He never finished taking off that T-shirt.

I was on him, ten years of that built-up rage pushing through my arms and into my fists. I beat his butt, no other way to put it. The police were called, and when they got there, my mom's boyfriend was a bloody mess, with his T-shirt still all rumpled up around his shoulders. He told the police that I was on drugs, and that's why I went so crazy. I guess they believed him, but only because they hadn't known him for ten years. But there was an ambulance there, too (for his whooped butt, not for mine), and the EMT checked me out.

"This kid isn't on anything, not even alcohol. He's clean."

And I was. My mom's boyfriend decided not to press charges. That's about as close as he ever came to admitting he was wrong.

I'll tell you, anybody that gets involved with a comedian has to have a little patience. Because we all have a touch of schizophrenia. If you can go through a bunch of stuff in your life and flip it into something funny, take all that pain and make it work for you, well, sometimes you're going to need your space, because sometimes that pain hits you and you can't flip it. You can't flip it into anything.

I was the only child my mother and father ever had. I required a lot of attention, and my mama gave it to me, every day. I don't mean she mothered me. What she did do was sit on the edge of my bed every night and ask me to tell her about my day before I went off to sleep. It was a way of saying we were still together, still a family, no matter what. Every day she did this, until I got to be a teenager and figured I didn't need that kind of attention anymore. How come we only see what we really needed as kids when we're too old to go back and get it?

My father was in the Air Force, and even before him **55**

and Mom split, I would only see him when he came home on leave. He was good to me, and years later, after I got famous, I looked him up. There were no hard feelings. Things go the way they go.

A while after my dad left for good, my mom lost her job at H.L. Greene department store in downtown Atlanta. Someone said she stole some money from the register. "I did not steal that money," she said to me, and I knew she was telling the truth—and not just because she's my mama. She had been earning seventy-five dollars a week, and she never got any child support money from my father. She's part of a generation that is no longer. The kind that knows how to bounce back, the kind that keeps being hardworking and honest and has that faith. She got herself a grant to go back to college, and earned a secretarial degree. Then, she worked for the Atlanta Police Department for a while, but watching them drag the criminals in night after night took its toll on her. Eventually, she settled into working at the Georgia Baptist Cleaning Service, and then did the cleaning work for Morris Brown University.

"I don't know how we're gonna make it, but we're gonna make it," she always said to me. And it wasn't easy. She got depressed, a lot of the times because of the way that boyfriend behaved. Looking back on it, it's amazing what she achieved, because she got through it all in spite of the depression and the poverty.

That spirit must have rubbed off on me. We sure had a bond, the two of us. If she had three dollars, she'd give me two. Many is the time I would hear her alone in her room at night, praying. Many is the time I would come home at night to find her sitting quietly in the dark after the lights, the phone, the gas had all been cut off.

I'd call out, "Mom, you home?"

"I'm here, honey."

We'd sit and talk, and I'd ask how much we owed. I had money, from some of the three different jobs I was doing to make ends meet. I'd hand her enough to pay those utilities, and even have enough left over for some groceries. And the dollar that was left, I'd press into her hand and say, "Hold this."

"Where are you getting this money?" Mom would want to know.

"I do work, around."

"Are you selling drugs?"

"No way."

"Good. Because your uncle would kill you if you were selling drugs, you know that. There are other things you can do to make money."

I surely knew that my uncle would kill me if I went near any drugs, and I surely knew about some of the other ways to make money.

Work to Do

J did any kind of job I could find. I bagged groceries at the Red Dot Supermarket, on Simpson Road, for $1.90 an hour. The toughest part about that job was when your friends came in, and you can see them as plain as day filling their pockets with red hots and Lemonheads, and then grabbing one piece of penny bubble gum and getting in line to pay just for THAT! I'm down the end of the counter bagging this lady's order, and there's my buddy, looking this way and that and whistling, knowing that I know that he knows that he's got a quarter's worth of candy in his pants. But he's there making a big show out of letting everybody notice that he intends to pay for ONE damn thing! And you can't snitch on your friends, right?

So, while you're walking that lady's groceries out to her car you get your buddy to walk beside you, and you tell him, "If you're gonna steal, go to another store!"

But now, you're worried that the manager might have

seen you talking to this kid, and if the manager places you with him, and the kid gets caught next time, then your job is over! This was some tricky have-to-play-it-just-right underworld *Godfather* game for an eleven-year-old to be dealing with!

And then you'd get the lady's cart full of groceries to her car, only to find that there's everything in the damn trunk but room. These old women from the town had the craziest bunch of crap in their trunks at all times. Five hundred church fans, a hundred prayer books, plus she just did four months' worth of laundry and that's bulging up in there, too. And you've got sixteen bags of groceries ("Be careful of the eggs, sonny.") to fit into this traveling damn storeroom ("No, no, that's bread, sonny, don't crush the bread.") and you've got to move around the church fans and the laundry ("Mind you don't spill anything on it.") to fit it all in. By the time you're done, you realize you probably would have broken less of a sweat if you just bench-pressed this lady all afternoon.

Then, when you've finally readjusted, rammed, and pushed everything into the trunk, you get the well-earned tip for your extra effort: a firm handshake and a "thank you." What the hell are you going to do? These are your elders. I wasn't the first bag boy to get a firm handshake for a tip, and I sure as hell would not be the last. You just didn't lip off to older people. I tried it once with Miss Thomas, and I learned my lesson.

Mrs. Thomas, wife of Mr. Taylor Thomas, asked if I would mow her lawn for four dollars. Before that, I had run errands for her. She always sent me to the store to get her a pack of Filter King Kools. You know, I've forgotten the names of women I've been with, but I will always remember those Filter King Kools. What the hell is up with that, anyway? Just like every time I went for those Kools, a dog named Butch would follow me there and back. Butch belonged to Li'l Albert Wilkins, who we called Big Albert. It's kind of beautiful the things you remember, isn't it?

Anyway, the Thomases' lawn was the size of a damn football field. Not only did I mow all of it, in the hot sun, but I took extra care, too. I raked up the leaves and put them in bags first. I trimmed the hedges, and cut back the plants. This was sure as hell more than a four-dollar job! So, when Mrs. Thomas came out to pay me, I told her all I had done, and said I thought it would be worth seven dollars to her.

"What?"

Her screwed-up face didn't worry me any. I took the gas cap off the lawn mower, and pointed inside. "This tank is empty, Mrs. Thomas. This lawn used up an entire tank of gasoline."

"You wait right here, young man."

Do you know, this woman went inside and called my *mother*?

"Mrs. Church, your boy is trying to charge me seven dollars for mowing the lawn."

Man, adults had this whole damn network at hand for messing up kids' plans! Of course, underneath it all there was this entire, very complex unspoken language that kicked in when grown-ups got that *you* got it. Mrs. Thomas did not pay me seven dollars. She paid me four, then asked me to stay for some of her homemade pound cake and some lemonade. Like I say, without words, she was telling me I had the right to ask for more money for the work I'd done, but that I hadn't paid enough dues yet to win the battle with someone many years older than me. I'll tell you, that pound cake was delicious. But the message from way back was just too strong to ignore: she's older, so you can't say nothing.

Cantrell's was a neighborhood store, restaurant, and pool hall, in the bluffs, on the corner of Kennedy Street and my street, Chestnut. There was only one way in and one way out, and Steve Cantrell always tried to make sure that either way you were going, it was going to be through him. There was always a fight to break up in the pool hall, and Steve would burst in like some *French Connection* renegade cop screaming, "Don't nobody move or I'll shoot everybody!" Unlike my uncle, you got the feeling that Steve Cantrell would do it. So then he would reach inside his jacket for the gun, but by the time he could get it, everyone would stampede past him and mow him down. Bad planning on Steve's part, there. Everybody knew there was only one way out of Cantrell's.

When I got tired of earning money doing odd jobs, I would bet on games of pool. I was only twelve years old, but I was really good at it. In fact, that night I gave my mother the money for the utility bills, I had just won a bundle shooting pool. Nobody seemed to mind that I was young. I never hustled anybody; when I won, I won fair and square. There was a guy named Donald Ham, we called him "Pledge" Ham (I don't remember why). Every time Pledge bet on me, I would lose for some reason. It got so people started knowing that, and I made him stop betting on me, so whoever I was playing wouldn't be sure they'd win. This drove Pledge crazy. "But if I *don't* bet on you, you're gonna win. It's not fair!"

Cantrell's had a few regulars who burned themselves

into my memory. "Cream" drove the neighborhood ice cream truck. He was tall and rangy, and he could shake the pinball machine without making it "tilt."

Mr. Sterling was a crusty old numbers runner, long since retired. Those days, he would make money by driving old ladies home from the market for five dollars. This was a pretty common occurrence in the Atlanta of my youth, and it was mostly the really elderly women who took advantage of it. The men used to say if they catch a woman of forty, they think they came up.

Miss Cantrell, the owner's sister, had a brother named Tatum Water. He was a mean, crazy drunk who hated kids, and didn't care if he told you so. Tatum would always wrangle a way to borrow money from Mr. Sterling, then spend it on liquor and never pay it back. Mr. Sterling kept saying he was keeping a careful record book of all of Tatum's defaulted loans.

"I'm keeping track, Tatum Water!" Sterling would yell at him.

"I'll slap you! I'll slap you!" Tatum would holler, and lean over like he was going to do it. Sterling would back off, but then they would start in again, and so it went on, back and forth, on and on, every day. At least that's the way we remember it, isn't it? Always repeating the same way.

The only guy in Cantrell's who could ever beat me at pool regularly was a Cherokee Indian whose name I'm afraid I do not recall. He would walk in real slow and say in that quiet, Indian way, "I'm looking for Li'l Bruce." I tried to find out why this man kept beating me. He told me that when you played pool against someone, "you got to get into their head." I figured out that by telling me that, he was getting into my head, all right. And he was good at it. So one night, I don't know how I managed it, I wouldn't let him in there. I blocked him out. And he could feel it, too. I just looked at him halfway through the game and said, "Okay, man. After this shot, I'm gonna run the table." And I did. I beat him that night. The mind is capable of some pretty amazing shit, isn't it?

The Dozens

art of growing up in the neighborhood was playing the dozens. It was one of the ways we kept the deep roots we came from in the front of our minds, by making a game out of insulting our friends. "You're so ugly, you couldn't get laid if you were a brick." Cracking and snapping on your friends was another way of bringing the love. And having an audience to hear your most creative insult made it all the sweeter. Playgrounds, street corners, chicken shacks, that's where we gathered. You lined up what aspect of your opponent's personality you wanted to bag on, and found the sharpest way you could to do just that. Only if things were getting desperate, if you were losing by several snaps, would you have to go to your last resort: cracking on somebody's mother. It was a dangerous move, but it could be effective if it was funny enough. "Your mother is so fat, she broke her arm and gravy poured out," for instance.

THE DOZENS APTITUDE TEST

Match the correct word or phrase below that correctly completes each dozens insult.

1. Your mother's so stupid, they say it's chilly outside, she brings out a _____.

2. Your brother's so fat, his talking scale says
"_____."

3. Your sister's so fat, she got stuck when she jumped up
_____.

4. Your brother's so fat, the police pulled him over and said, "_____."

5. Your lips are so big, you can whisper in your
_____.

6. You're so ugly, they can press your face into dough and make _____ cookies.

7. Your sister is so skinny, her bra fits _____.

8. You're so ugly, your dad came to the hospital with toys, but when he saw you he took 'em back and got a
_____.

9. You're so ugly you have to trick-or-treat
_____.

10. You're so stupid, it takes you an hour to cook
_____.

A. own ear
B. over the phone
C. better backward
D. bowl and spoon
E. cage
F. One person at a time
G. Minute rice
H. unknown gorilla
I. in the air
J. Everybody out of the car

Answers: 1.D, 2.F, 3.I, 4.J, 5.A, 6.H, 7.C, 8.E, 9.B, 10.G

HOW DID YOU SCORE?

None wrong:
You're so smart, Einstein says, "What the hell you talking about?"

Two wrong:
You're not smart enough to pass a blood test.

Three to five wrong:
Men: You probably think Taco Bell is a Mexican phone book.
Women: You will most likely ask a baker about your yeast infection.

Five to eight wrong:
If you spoke your mind, you'd be speechless.

More than eight wrong:
When you were born, your mother slapped the doctor.

The Granddaddy of
Them All

Sometimes I visit elementary schools, talking to young children about what it takes to make it in this world. They all figure that since Bruce Bruce has hung out with Lil Jon and the Ying Yang Twins, that he can tell them what it's like to have all that money, and be in the videos with the girls and the cars.

First they ask, "Are you married?" Then it's "Do you have five girlfriends? I'm gonna have me five girlfriends when I grow up."

Then it's "What kind of car you drive over here in?" When I answer, damn straight it wasn't what they were expecting. "You rode the BUSSSS?"

See, I try to tell these kids that any job is hard work. That even a lot of the rappers they see on TV are still struggling. They're working long hours to make those videos, and the cars and the mansions and the pools they're playing in are rented. The women are actresses, also working hard for their pay. All of this is used to put a certain image out there, and a lot of young people think that the rented props and the paid extras are things that they will have EVERY DAY when they make it big. I don't blame them for thinking that, but I know that I would have been able to tell the difference between something being sold to me and something I had to work for. That's because I was lucky. I came up in a time when home training was still important.

These days, kids don't understand the difference between watching the video and actually living it. Nowadays, you have to be careful how you speak to young players. Make sure you're friendly, be casual. "Everything a'ight? What's up, man, one love, know what I'm sayin'?" Because young boys now, they got something for you. You know what I mean. *Come a little closer to the Suburban, and we got somethin' for ya. . . .*

You have to be real nice to young players today. "Hey, brother, how you doin'? Ain't nothin' but love. What's happenin'?"

Man, if they get you outside, it's, "Why don't you come on over here, I'll show you what's happenin'."

Young men don't play anymore. It's not like when I was young. We'd talk, and then fight. These young boys shoot, and then ride out. No talking or fighting!

But when my mama whooped me, I GOT IT. I knew I'd done something wrong. Before my mom and dad split, when my dad would be home on leave from the Air Force, he would always get some kind of job while he was home. One time, he worked for the Atlanta Police Department and they gave him a gun. I could not take my eyes off that weapon. When my daddy saw this, he grabbed me hard by the shoulders.

"Look at me," he told me. "Do not play with this gun."

Let me tell you, that threat was so DEEP. Soooo deep! There was no question that you were never going to play with that gun. This wasn't like in some scary movie, where the guy says, "Whatever you do, do not open that door," and after a while you can't help yourself, you just have to open that door. Your elders told you something, that was IT. You were not tempted to disobey them, because you respected them as folks who have already been where you are going. Mind you, me and my best buddy Barry played *all around* that gun. We got it out of my daddy's closet and put it on the floor. Then, we took our GI Joes and our toy Jeeps and moved them all around the room, running figure eights on either side of the gun that was lying right there in front of us.

"You touched the gun."

"The hell I did."

"Your army man touched the gun."

"You drove your tank right over the gun, I saw you!"

But we *did not play with that gun*! That's how it was back in the day. There were things you did not do. You did not talk back, and you did not cuss in front of church. Every kid knew it, and since kids follow what other kids do, that was just how it was.

That's why I say, to anybody who has any children nowadays, start in early and beat them. Go home, wake them up, beat them. They have done something you don't know about.

And you do not have to reason with a child. You are the parent, and what you say, GOES. Oh, and white people? Quit making deals with your kids. "All right, Brandon, I'll let you watch television if you promise to wash the dishes at least once a week, I mean, if it's not too much trouble, sweetheart, okay?" I'm here to tell you, you do not have to make a deal with your child.

My mother used to make a deal with me. She'd say, "Boy, cut the front yard. When you get through, don't forget the back. And that's the damn DEAL!"

My mama didn't play. She was one of those mothers that used to threaten you before you go anywhere.

She'd say, "Bruce, we're going to Kmart, and DON'T ASK ME FOR NOTHING!"

Man, I'd see a toy fire truck I wanted so bad. I'd start making little motions toward it, grabbing up at the shelf where it was, hoping somebody would notice.

My dad asked me, "Do you see something you want, Bruce?"

"Yeah," I told him, "but Mama told me don't ask her for nothing."

"She did? Damn, boy, you're trying to get us both messed up!"

My uncle, he was able to discipline me, to give me that good home training, because I didn't want to make him mad enough to kill me, even though I knew he wouldn't kill me. My grandfather, Alex Church, my mother's father, now he was a different story. I *feared* that man, plain and simple.

Even when he was old and couldn't bathe himself anymore, my granddad was one damn imposing man. Everything about him scared me, and it started with his voice. Low, but clear, it sounded like his belly was a cave and there was a bear in there waiting to get out. He could speak two words—"come here"—and I'd be shaking in my boots. Then he'd lean back, pull up his pant legs, and say

what he had to say.

"If I start whooping you right now, it'll take seven doctors whistlin' 'Dixie' with saltine crackers in their mouth and no water to pull me off your butt."

And most of the time, there wasn't anything pissing him off more than he'd run out of potato pie. At Grandma Mertie's house, it was MANDATORY to have something sweet around at all times.

"If you see me running out of cakes," Granddad would say, "I would advise you to start cooking some more."

Damn! And don't ask him to repeat himself. He tells you something ONE TIME, and you better take it in.

"I don't chew my cabbage twice, boy," that's what he'd always say.

And this man was LAZY! He wasn't going to do shit, and he was not ashamed to tell you so. He worked at Rexall Drugs, as a maintenance man.

"What'd you do today, Grandpa?"

"I didn't do a damn thing. I supervised."

On the weekends, he was a jackleg preacher. He'd go do a revival, get everyone all fired up with the good works of the Lord, then he'd take the collection money and disappear for a while. The church folk would be calling the house, "Is the deacon there?" He didn't care, he was just messing with them. You just did not want to get into any drama with Granddad.

That voice of his could even put a scare into his hogs.

My grandma and granddad had a salt house, where you cure meat. They would raise a hog until it weighed eight hundred pounds, and Granddad told everyone that he wouldn't take the hog for killing until it started getting cool. I was sitting on the porch with him in the early part of the fall, and we weren't too far from that old hog in his pen. Within earshot of that hog, my granddaddy just said two words, like when he would only have to say two words to me to get me shaking. He said them like he was just talking, like he was just commenting on the weather, but those words came from that same cave inside his belly, and they carried the same threat.

"Gettin' cool," was all he said.

That hog started squealing, spinning around in a circle, trying to get out of the yard. He knew, brother, he knew his number was up soon! His piggy brain zeroed right in on what Granddad was getting at.

Like with most kinds of fear, it's mixed in with respect, too. There were things about spending time with my mom's folks that had magic in them. To talk about them now, I feel like they are times that must not seem real to people my kids' age. Like some kind of scene in a movie where they put that orange-colored filter over the lens and everything looks like one of those old photographs, the kind you couldn't just take to the drugstore to get developed.

Down in Grandma's root cellar were jars of preserves made out of grapes from the muscadine vines around the house. That woman jarred everything. There were jars of string beans in that cellar that wouldn't go bad for years once she sealed them up. I loved going out to pick the grapes off those muscadine vines. I came across a rattlesnake in there once, and froze up.

My granddad saw me go all still and said, "You scared, Bruce? Come on, you're big enough to go bear hunting with a switch!"

I didn't say anything. I just stayed scared. Granddad

grabbed that snake by its neck with his bare hands and smashed it dead. He kept the snake skin as a souvenir.

As tough as Granddad was, there was a day when I thought for sure he was going to come in second place. It was 1969. I was still a small boy. My uncle Paul got ahold of a 1966 Impala, and, man, he wanted to drive that machine around so badly that he figured he would drive it without getting insurance. Granddaddy Church figured he should set Paul straight on this matter.

Now, down in the South, there's an unspoken thing that you can still get a whooping from your elders when you're twenty-three, twenty-four years old. Because old people didn't play. Like I told you, my granddad was the type of person who would say something . . .

. . . one time.

That's it. That's the way it goes. So my granddaddy pulled up those pant legs the way he did, and he shifted that old body from side to side, saying, "Look here, boy. Y'all don't need to be driving that car, unless you get some insurance."

My uncle was a twenty-three-year-old man. He knew about the unspoken whooping rule, but he didn't care, because he was young and strong, so he lipped off. "You can't tell me what to do, I'm grown. I'm twenty-three years old."

"Boy, you ain't drivin' that car until you get yourself some insurance."

"Hell with you. I can drive my car any way I want."

My granddaddy shifts his weight again and says, "Let me get through eatin' this potato pie, then you tell me what you feel about that car."

I'm watching this and I'm thinking, "Oh, boy, my poor **77** granddaddy is going to get his butt WHOOPED!" Those two minutes it took him to finish that potato pie went in slow motion. I was watching that mouth of his, while it let that pie dissolve in there, then finally that last big swallow. That Adam's apple working up and down. Granddad set down the plate, put the fork on top of it. I still remember that sound, like the opening bell of a prize fight.

"You gonna drive that car any way you want, that what you're tellin' me?"

"That's right," said my uncle.

The two men squared off, and Paul didn't barely raise his arm before Granddad popped him right in the mouth! Man, my uncle never recovered! A twenty-three-year-old man getting beaten down by a guy twenty-five years his senior. And my grandma's in the house watching the whole thing. You know what she said? Nothing. This was something between these two men. Besides, Granddad knew that later on, when the house was quiet and they were both in bed, she would approach him about her feelings. That was how it was done, in the privacy of their bedroom, behind closed doors. I was staying with them that night, and I had to go to the bathroom after midnight. I walked by my grandparents' room, and sure enough Grandma was airing her opinion on the day's whooping. I could hear her as I walked by.

All she said was, "You didn't have to hit him all in the head like that."

My grandpa said, "Too bad. I'm the one taught him to fight, and dammit, he shouldn't have dropped that left! Every time he did he just left me open to jab the shit out of him."

You know how those old men were. The way things

were back in the day. We had to go buy a refrigerator one time, and my granddad didn't want to know any other store but Sears. My granddaddy walked in there with my grandma and me. And if that day was a scene in a movie, it would have played something like this:

INT. SEARS / APPLIANCE DEPARTMENT—DAY

Grandma and Granddaddy Church walk into the appliance section with young Bruce, age nine. Grandma looks with excitement at all the refrigerators around her.

Grandma
I want to take awhile and look at some of these refrigerators.
Granddaddy walks over to a big white refrigerator with a freezer door on top.

Granddaddy
I don't care what you look at. This is the one we're getting right here. The white one.

Grandma
Well, I'm gonna look around and see what I can find.
Young Bruce looks up at his grandparents. Grandaddy pulls up his pant legs and points again to the big white fridge.

Granddaddy
I don't give a damn where you look! That's the one we're getting.
A salesman approaches.

Salesman
May I help you, ma'am?

Grandma

We're in the market for a new refrigerator.

The salesman walks Grandma over to a shiny red model.

Salesman

How about this fine quality refrigerator right here, ma'am? This is a brand-new style. Double doors!

Grandma

Well, I . . .

Grandma glances over at Granddaddy, who meets her eye and says nothing!

Grandma

(seeing the look Granddaddy is giving her)

. . . No. Not that one. But let me look at some of the other ones you have here.

Grandma starts walking around the show floor with the salesman. Grandaddy pulls young Bruce over to him.

Granddaddy

Come and sit down, Bruce. You and me are gonna be here awhile.

ONE OF THOSE LONG WAVY DISSOLVE EFFECTS TAKES US TO THE SAME PLACE IN THE SEARS STORE—45 MINUTES LATER.

Young Bruce and Granddaddy look up as Grandma returns with the salesman.

Salesman

So, what do you think, ma'am?

Grandma walks over to the big white fridge that her husband had pointed to at the beginning, almost an hour ago. She points to it.

Grandma
We'll take this white one.

Salesman
A good choice.
Granddad stands up with young Bruce.

Granddaddy
Damn, woman.

END OF SCENE

For Real Jobs, for Real Family

*A*round the time of my fourteenth birthday, I figured it was time to look for some kind of employment a little more stable than shooting pool. When I decided to apply at the Old Hickory House, a steak house in Buckhead, I didn't know I would be starting a career I would have until I was twenty-four years old. What young man thinks about being twenty-four when he's only fourteen anyway?

When Eddie Wise, the manager of the Old Hickory House, interviewed me, he asked me outright: "How old are you, son?"

"I'm fourteen, sir," I told him. I couldn't lie. And I was old enough now that it wasn't just because I thought my uncle would shoot everybody if I did. It was just a part of me now, not lying. But, I figured I'd blown it, because in Atlanta you had to be sixteen to get a job like this.

"You know what?" said Eddie Wise. "I'm gonna give you this job because you didn't lie to me."

He started me at $2.90 an hour. Every day I left school at three thirty on the west side, caught the bus through downtown into Buckhead, got to the Old Hickory House at four thirty, did my homework there until five thirty, then went to work.

I began as a busboy. My first few days there, I would go to clear the dishes into my bus bucket, and there would be money left behind on the table. I couldn't imagine what the hell it was doing there. Miss Lucy was one of those gum-smacking, heart-of-gold waitresses like you see in the movies, the kind who maybe got burned by some man long ago but she ain't gonna let that bother her, and here she is like always, working at the diner. She'd already been working at the Hickory House forever when I started there.

"Miss Lucy?" I stopped her sometime during my first week bussing tables. "Why do people keep leaving money on the table?"

"What's that, Bruce?" she asked me. "You mean you don't know what a tip is?"

"No, ma'am."

"And you just saw this money on the table every time and didn't say anything?"

"That's right. What's a tip?"

"Young man, you are so damn honest it's scary."

I still remember Miss Lucy walking away that day, her voice trailing off behind her as she went into the kitchen saying, "Did you hear what that cute little boy just asked me. . . . ?"

Before long I was washing dishes, and inside of a year

I was working the grill. My uncle had taught me how to cook, and I couldn't wait to make use of the training.

Frank ran the barbecue pit on the night shift. He cooked all the meat. He had cerebral palsy in his left hand, and it made him insecure about keeping his job, so he always talked to me like I was going to mess things up for him.

"What you doin', Bruce? Go clean the bathroom, do something."

"All right, all right," I'd tell him.

"My name is Frank," he would say. "The F mean 'f— you up.'"

When Frank moved to another store, Curtis Copeland took over. He called himself "Sweet T." Sweet T was my man. He had tie-tongue, a harelip, but it did not stop him from being a player.

"How y'all doin'? I'm Sweet T. Y'all like iced tea, right? Well, that's me. The best iced tea there is. Sweet T. What's your zodiac sign, honey? You're a Virgo? Oh, baby, that's perfect. I'm a Pisces. I figure you and me are compatible."

At school, I was always talking, but I froze up when it came down to it. But Sweet T was *smooth*. He'd see a pretty woman arrive on her own, and pretend like he hadn't been bird-dogging her since she walked through the door.

"Welcome to Old Hickory House, darlin'. You and your man gonna eat good tonight? What's that? You ain't got no man tonight? Whaaat? A fine . . . intelligent . . . good-looking lady like yourself?"

God bless Sweet T.

Eventually, I became a food expediter, which meant I made up the plates and the sandwiches. I took over the night shift from Fast Eddie ("Wassup, young man?") when he moved to days. "Watch me now, Bruce!" Eddie would call out, and I did. But I made the job my own. I took pride in cooking a good steak. Customers would call me on the phone, asking, "Are you cooking fresh ribs tonight? You are? When will they be ready? Just tell me what time to come in!"

"Don't burn that steak, now, you hear?"

"Where's my sizzle? That steak better be sizzlin' when I get it!"

"Gimme some of that coleslaw!"

One gentleman used to come by the Old Hickory House just to find out when I would be working. I regret that I never knew his name. He sounded like he might have been from Germany. I wasn't too curious about such things in my teens. What I do remember was that he drove a 1970 Buick Wildcat. Miss Lucy would say, "That guy came by again. All he wanted to know was 'When will Bruce be here?' I told him to come back tonight." He always ordered the same thing. Most people got to liking things done the same way. His was a chopped steak, medium well. Looking back on it, this guy was my first big fan, only he kept coming back for the food and not the comedy.

The owner of the Old Hickory House chain was a man named Jack Black. We liked each other right away. His company was family owned, and we shared a lot of the same philosophy of work and life. Right when I started working for Old Hickory House, he brought me on to do the yard work at his house. I'd do any kind of task around the place that he needed; sweeping, watering plants. He kept meticulous track of my hours, and paid me fairly. I worked for him for ten years.

By the time I was twenty, I was moved to another Old Hickory House, where I ran the pit. This was a high-volume store that saw thirty thousand dollars a week. The manager was an ex-Navy man named Jerry, and he was not an easy man to get along with. If everything wasn't just his definition of perfect, he wouldn't hesitate to cuss out me, or anyone else. But Jerry liked me. He said I was conscientious, and he made me assistant manager. We had a branch concession in the lounge at the Atlanta Speedway, and I'd work there sometimes, cooking steaks for Richard Petty. But Jerry would talk trash about Mr. Black behind his back, and this started getting to me.

Jerry's sister went and married another guy named Jerry, and that Jerry started a restaurant called Jerry's Lucky Street Grille. My Jerry took over the place from his sister's husband Jerry in 1985, and left the Old Hickory House. (It's only two Jerrys, but it seems like a hell of a lot more, doesn't it?) My Jerry asked me to come and work for him. I left Old Hickory House and followed him to Lucky Street, but before too long I was unhappy. So, I quit.

The minute after I gave notice, I called Mr. Black. He was glad I called. I went back to work at his home for several more years. I will never regret my time cooking steaks and making people happy that way. There are all kinds of job satisfaction. I get a lot of joy out of what I do now, making a lot of people laugh, but it means even more because I can see it as another step on my journey. It will never cancel out all the great things that came before. Anyway, without my varied job experience, I would have had a lot less people to mark, and a lot less material.

I also would not have had much of an income, which would not have sat well with my uncle, since I had a wife and three children of my own to support by now.

* * *

Let me tell you, my ex-wife got mean when she was pregnant. You hear about women's moods changing when they're carrying a baby inside of them, but this was straight out of *The Exorcist*. She could have floated six inches above the bed and I wouldn't have batted an eye. And you can't lip off a pregnant woman! She's got all this hormonal stuff going on, so it's not her fault, right? Damn! We went to see the doctor when her mood swings got really bad.

The doctor took me aside and said, "Bruce, the only thing to do is to keep her calm."

I said, "Calm? Doc, if she cusses me one more time, I'll jump on her and the damn baby!"

If my children were here right now, I would proudly say that my daughter and my two sons are the biggest blessings I have ever had in my life, and that I love them more than anything in this world.

Our first two children were boys. It might have ended there, but I cannot forget the cold chill that went through me that morning when we all sat down to breakfast, and my then-wife said:

"Wouldn't it be nice if we had a little girl?"

For the first years of their lives, the only way I would hold my children would be while I was sitting still in a chair, with the chair back flat against the wall. I was scared! I thought I would break these little things! And I would not allow a babysitter, I was way too protective for that. It worked out fine, since when I couldn't be with the children, I would just make their mother stay home with them. She didn't mind this at all, because she refused to work anyway. Her staying at home with the kids was the only subject we didn't yell about.

Those kids went everywhere with me, even to the junkyard. I'd tell them what the car part I needed looked like, and we'd all poke around looking for the thing. Some psychologist reading this might say that I never let my kids be alone because I had some kind of unhealthy attachment issue. My kids turned out fine. I was just a little overly concerned for their safety. I wanted to make sure they weren't going to be fools their whole life, like me. Yeah, it ended up working out for me, but let's face it, it could have gone either way for a boy who threw rocks up in the air to see what they looked like coming down. And my oldest, he's the sneaky one. He pulled a lot of the same kind of stunts I did when I was a boy, only he got away with them, because his daddy kept hearing that voice saying, "Leave him alone, he's creative." I figured I would cure him of the need to go joyriding at the age of ten like I did, and I just let him drive all the time when we went out. With me supervising, of course. He was very serious about it. He knew I trusted him, and he trusted me. To tell you the truth, I let all my kids drive the car with me while they were little. Remembering how my daughter looked while she raised her head over the top of that steering wheel still brings me joy. You could say I was reckless, but nowadays things have gotten too restricted. The way to protect your children is to know what they're doing, when they're with you and when they can't be with you. Getting involved in their lives, even if it's to do something a little crazy, that's how you protect them.

My little girl, she might as well have been the real mother figure in the house. She made sure her brothers were taken care of, but make no mistake, she got taken care of first. And I couldn't do anything about it. It doesn't matter if it's a daughter, a wife, or a girlfriend. If it's a female, she's got you wrapped around that little finger.

She'd be chewing a piece of gum and say, "Daddy, my brothers need gum, too. And they sure ain't gettin' mine."

Sometimes, being around kids takes you right back to when you were one, and you screw up just like you did when you were their age. My baby boy, the middle child, when he was four years old he wanted goldfish so badly he could bust. Finally, I saved up enough to get him an aquarium with all kinds of fish in it. Everything was cool, until he reminded me that the man at the pet store told him he has to have a grown-up change the water in the aquarium. I didn't know shit about aquariums, so I changed out the old water with hot water from the tap that came out way too hot. Those fish went belly-up in half an hour, and he went running around the house screaming, "My daddy is a murderer! My daddy is a murderer!"

Of course, like most everything when you're four, he forgot and moved on to something else. Kids don't remember what they do, but adults do. This was the same kid that stored up an extra stream of pee to shoot out just when I was changing his diaper.

And Baby Boy HATED his sister when she was born! "She's not my sister," that's what he would say, whenever he was around her. One day, I saw this two-year-old swinging his baby sister's bassinet like he was David getting ready to slingshot Goliath. That girl's eyes were open wide, and her arms were flying out in front of her, wondering what kind of ride she was getting taken on. But what my son didn't know was that I went and checked with the doctor about how he wasn't getting along with his new sister, and the doctor told me to let the boy help every time I did anything for my baby girl. Before long, that child was jumping out of his chair when she needed anything. "I'll get the Pampers!"

Then there was the time my daughter threatened Santa Claus. It started when we went to the fair, and she saw a pony in the petting zoo.

"Look at that big dog over there!" She was not the brightest child.

When she found out it was a pony, she wanted one so badly she could bust. So when we went to see Santa Claus down at the mall, she told him he better get her a pony, because if he didn't, she would tell her daddy and her daddy would whoop his butt.

That's the crazy thing about being a father, though. If your daughter really needs you to open a can of whoop-ass on anybody, even Santa Claus, chances are you'll do it.

Bring in the Chips, Bring in the Funny

I'm real glad that I found my way into show business through real life. It's your real life experiences that make you who you are. How can you keep it real if you've never had a real life before you go up there on that stage? And it wouldn't be too long now before I did get on up there.

My next opportunity to start marking folks came when I worked for Frito-Lay. Man, I did a show every morning there, while I was loading up my truck with bags of chips to take to stores all around Atlanta. I'd clown around on the loading dock, doing imitations of everybody.

"That damn Bruce," was something I heard all the time at Frito-Lay.

I got to meet people like Roger, a white guy who prided himself on hanging out with the brothers, only he tried too hard to show it. Roger wore bell-bottoms and looked like he stopped paying attention to how black people dressed back around 1971, during the *Shaft/Foxy Brown* years.

Then there was Larry, who told jokes, like old-school jokes that you didn't want to laugh at, but you just had to.

"Hey, Bruce!"

"Yeah, Larry."

"Did you hear about them two stores that merged?"

"No, Larry, which two stores?"

"The Stop 'N Go and the A&P."

"For real, Larry?"

"Yeah. The new store's called the "Stop & Pee.""

Larry had this other joke he always told that never really made any sense to me, mostly because he never carried a cow leg to start with.

"Hey, Bruce, do you know why I carry a cow leg?"

"No, Larry, why you carry a cow leg?"

"Because it keeps the gorillas away."

"Okay, Larry."

"Do you see any gorillas around here, Bruce?"

"No, Larry."

"Then it's workin', ain't it?"

My job took me to 7-Elevens, Wal-Marts, grocery stores. They called it "route sales." Most of the managers at these establishments would end their day around three thirty in the afternoon, so they wanted their deliverymen to get there by around a quarter to three, to give them time to rotate out the stock, take care of the paperwork, and let the manager sign off on it before three thirty.

Bob Wade had the last store on my route, and I could never get there early enough for him. He wanted to leave way before three thirty, but I hardly ever got there in time for him to do that. And this man had no sense of humor. I didn't even want to know who put what foreign object up his ass way back when. I tried to play it cool around him, because route sales guys could get in trouble if they got the managers riled up. Like I say, I *tried* to play it cool around Bob, for as long as I could.

Until that one day.

I busted my butt on the route, and I got to Bob's store way early, at two twenty in the afternoon. And he sees me coming, and he starts *applauding*. You know, whacking his palms together, making a big deal out of me showing up before three, making sure all of his employees can see.

"Weh-hell," he says. "That's more like it."

I didn't say anything, just went and rotated out the stock. Then, as we're wrapping up the paperwork, I couldn't help myself. It just came out:

"You know, Bob, I heard a joke yesterday that's so funny it will take the hair off your head. Oh, I see you've already heard it."

Bob went stone-faced, and he didn't say anything.

Next day, that voice came over the PA in the loading dock:

"Bruce, need to see you in the office."

I heard that voice more times than I can count. There was the time I pointed out to James Pike, the manager of a Wal-Mart on my route, that the madder he got, the lower he talked. Have you ever known anyone like that? I can imagine how that would mess with some poor older person.

"What?"

(Sounds like silence with a little air blowing through it.)

"What?"

(More silence with a little air blowing through it.)

"Damn it, I could swear I saw your lips move."

Anyway, I guess I wasn't supposed to say anything about stuff like that. And sure enough, Bob Wade had called my supervisor about the "take the hair off your head" joke. Like with most situations in life, you can lose your damn job if you have too much personality.

I stayed on best behavior, but a few weeks later, that voice came over the PA again:

"Bruce, need to see you in the office."

Everyone on the loading dock looked at me.

"Damn!" I said. "What I done did now?"

The whole way up to see my supervisor, I was going over in my mind who I could have pissed off. Then, I stepped into the supervisor's office, and if it was a scene in a movie, it would have gone something like this:

INT. FRITO-LAY SUPERVISOR'S OFFICE—DAY

Bruce enters. Behind a desk sits Jeff Massey, a supervisor in a short-sleeved shirt and bad tie.

Jeff
Bruce. Come on in and sit down.
Bruce pulls up a chair, sits across from Jeff.

Bruce
What'd I do, Jeff?

Jeff
Nothing, Bruce.

Bruce
Why am I here, then?

Baby James Brown

Jeff
You know that every year, the Stop 'N Go sponsors a contest to pick the best potato chip displays in all their stores around greater Atlanta?

Bruce
Yeah.

Jeff
I'm pleased to inform you, Bruce, that you have won first prize. A check for five thousand dollars.

Bruce
Five grand. I can sure use that for my wife and babies. Who won second prize?

Jeff
You did, Bruce. A camcorder and two color television sets.

Bruce
Whoa. I don't know what to say.

Jeff
Don't say anything, Bruce. Third prize is a trip to England.

Bruce
Who won that?

Jeff
You did, Bruce.

Bruce
Damn.

Jeff
My sentiments exactly, Bruce. Those are the top three prizes for the Stop 'N Go contest. They did also give out a fourth prize.

Bruce
What is it?

Jeff
It's a solitaire diamond ring, Bruce. Guess who won that?

Bruce
Me?

Jeff
Right you are, young man. You won the first, second, third, and fourth prizes. Damn incredible.

Bruce
Did you just cuss, sir?

Jeff
I wouldn't normally, Bruce, but this is your memory, so anything goes.

Bruce
Right on.

Everything but my supervisor cussing is true. I went and sold that trip to England, and the camcorder. Yeah, all right, and the diamond ring. I sold that, too. I kept the money and the TVs. You might think, now that I'm a celebrity, and I can get a table at all the good restaurants, and I know other famous people, and I'm doing all right, that I wouldn't even remember something like winning all four prizes in some little potato-chip display contest. But I will never forget it. It reminds me of how I got to where I am, how it's good to take pride in what you do. It reminds me of the good sense I got handed down to me in my home training. And it reminds me that there 98 are all kinds of victories and blessings in life. You all should keep an eye out for those ones that have come your way.

Now, all this time at Frito-Lay, my friends are telling me, "Bruce, you need to go on the stage." As far as I was concerned, I lived my whole life on a kind of stage, and it had never hit me that there was another level to take it to. You hear a lot of people referred to as "comedians" in life, and that doesn't mean they're doing it professionally. Me, I watched TV all the time. I loved Flip Wilson and Richard Pryor and *Sanford & Son* and Eddie Murphy and Martin Lawrence, and I knew I loved comedy; it was a big influence on the way I lived my life. Now, it was threatening to become a way of life. My way of life. I guess everything had fallen into place without me knowing it.

Open mike night at the Comedy Act Theatre in Atlanta was on a Tuesday, and all I'm thinking is, "I hope the people like me." But as soon as I hit the stage, I knew it was where I was supposed to be. This was where I was being led, from my James Brown impersonation to the roller coaster on Chestnut Street to lipping off Bob Wade.

Things got off to a rocky start, though. I got to the club and put my name on the list. I saw that I was number four to go up. But the host, Chris Charles, the "Chocolate Hippy," he kept skipping me. He would look down at my name and just skip over it. He didn't know me, and everyone else on the list was his boy, so he was going to bring them up. He played dumb, like he wasn't messing with me. I never went on that first night.

Or the second night, or the third night.

On the fourth night, the Chocolate Hippy finally picks my number, but decides to dog me out before I come up. **99**

"This next guy waiting to come on is a fat boy, look like he got some honey buns in his hand already."

I let it slide. I took the stage. Here were the first words out of my mouth:

"You know, I heard what the man said about the honey buns. But I've been looking at this here Chocolate Hippy, and where I come from, we'd call him the Chocolate Sissy."

Okay, not very original, I know, but cut me some slack, I was young and pissed off.

There was a *whoa* from the crowd—I swear I could feel their breath hit me like a gust of wind. They were thinking, "Who is this fat boy dissing on the host, and what the hell is going to happen as a consequence?"

The Chocolate Hippy walked back toward me, made like he was trying to grab the microphone away. I danced back and forth, wouldn't let him get ahold on it.

"I think today," I said, "you have met your match."

From the audience came a *Whoo-hooooo!* of "I can't believe he said that."

I started in. "I don't have but five minutes, so I better get on with it." I told stories about my uncle, about church, about redneck truckers. Better versions of one or two of the stories are still in the act today. Chocolate Hippy hung back, let me do my thing, saw that the crowd was laughing. A lot. When they gave me a standing ovation for my very first time on stage, that Hippy came back up to host, took the mike from me and sounded a lot less harsh than when we'd begun our little back-and-forth.

"You know what?" he said to the audience. "He's funny."

Before long, the people in the club were asking, "When that big guy coming back?"

And I did come back, every Tuesday. For my first few times out, I never held the microphone in my hands, I just stood behind the mike stand doing my act. That was when Gary Williams, the owner of the Comedy Act, Atlanta's first black comedy club, came over and took me by the shoulders.

"Get loose," he said, "let people see you."

I did, and he started me in on hosting Tuesday nights. This was a big thing for me. But, what I consider my first really big gig came awhile later. Through these early shows at the Comedy Act, I had made friends with other comedians. One of them, a female comic named Chocolate, had been lined up to do a big show in Savannah sponsored by Bonner Brothers Hair Products. They put on big events, evenings of comedy and gospel, with a thousand people in attendance. Chocolate decided to give me a shot. She said she didn't need the three hundred dollars, and even gave me her spot, and her round-trip ticket to Savannah (back when you could give someone else your airline ticket).

This was my very first show on a Saturday night, with a packed house! I spent the whole damn evening standing in the back by myself, scared to death! I don't even remember what I thought or did when I went out there and did my ten minutes. I remember that the people in the audience showed me love, and some of them even asked to have their picture taken with me afterward. Plus, the people at Bonner Brothers gave me two hundred dollars extra. Five hundred dollars! My first big paycheck! The minute I got back to Atlanta, I found Chocolate and thanked her. No matter what you do in life, you need people who believe in you. She was one of those people.

Now that I've got you all caught up in my amazing damn rags-to-riches story, let me check in with you on one important detail. See, the other thing I had to do upon returning to Atlanta was report for work at Frito-Lay. That's right. I had a family to support, and I still needed a steady job. And maybe doing comedy had set something exciting in motion, because the most exciting thing that might ever happen to a potato chip deliveryman was still waiting in the wings for me.

One day, while I was setting out my chips at a Wal-Mart, in Morrow, Georgia, someone called out, "Bruce, catch that girl!"

Before I go on, here is how it all started, which I learned later, after I was down on the ground gasping for breath: now, the store security guard at this Wal-Mart was a lady who liked to do "undercover" stuff, you know, pretending she's just shopping. I guess it made her job more exciting. I can see that. It's better than sitting on your butt in a metal folding chair looking like somebody who would be no problem at all to blow by on your way out of the store with half the merchandise. So, security lady is posing as a customer, pushing her shopping cart around, when she sees a young lady holding a baby, and reaching around the jewelry counter to steal a ring while the clerk has her back turned. Well, security lady gets up in the young lady's face, and the young lady starts fighting her! She's holding a baby, and beating the security lady! Joe, the guy who worked in the toy department putting bicycles together, he told me later that the ring stealer was coming out like Sugar Ray, jabbing and bobbing, and *BAM*! So, the security lady goes down, and then Joe sees ring stealer coming right at him.

"I'll get her!" he calls out, and that's when I turn around and see *him* getting bopped, and I mean bopped hard, by the ring stealer! It only took but one right hook. She just cold-cocked him while the baby's in her left arm, not making a sound. Joe drops like a sack of potatoes. Then the voice yells:

"Bruce! Catch that girl!"

I dropped my boxes of chips and took off running. I mean RUNNING! And I'm yelling to the ring stealer, "You need to stop!" And now she's hit the parking lot and I'm booking after her! And I hear someone behind me saying, "Look at the big guy run!"

And I'm caught up in it, man. I'm MOVING! Twenty years ago, I was running *from* a fifth-grade grade girl, and what goes around comes around, because now I am running *after* a full-grown woman. That's right, honey! I'm coming to get you, ring stealer! I'm flying, man, I'm Bruce Jenner! And then, over the next maybe thirty seconds, suddenly I am just not Bruce Jenner anymore. I am the furthest thing from Bruce Jenner. My body was suddenly telling me, "All right, son, you gave it your best shot, but you are a very large man and I'm about done here." Inside my brain, my footsteps are hissing down, slower and slower and slower. The inside of my body sounds like Darth Vader dying. I hear my heart pounding, and I can't breathe right anymore. My hands go to my knees, and then my knees drop to the pavement. I'm a wheezing mess.

I must have really looked like I was going to buy the damn farm, because the next thing I know, the ring stealer has come back to see if I'm all right! Her and her damn baby are helping *me* up!

"Are you okay?"

I'm breathing hard. "Lady, I'm just the Frito-Lay guy."

"I'm sorry."

At this point, I still don't know why they were after this girl. So I say, "Look, I don't know what they want with you, but I can just tell 'em I didn't catch you."

"There, there," she says, and rubs her hand up and down on my shoulder. I can't believe this. I'm being comforted by the felon who was trying to get away from me. And I guess it was her own fault for caring, because in the time it took her to help me up, a police car showed up. The cop that got out of that car was one of those guys who has to stick his big old meaty hand out onto the roof to help himself out. You think he's going to ruin the suspension just by exiting his own vehicle. He walks over to the ring stealer and that was that. She's in handcuffs.

The cop looks down at me and says, "Thanks for your help."

By the time I caught my breath enough to say "No problem," he had already walked away.

Back at the Frito-Lay loading dock, things weren't the same after my show in Savannah. There were no words spoken, but I was getting the message that those in authority had become resentful of my talent, and what little success I had been achieving with my comedy. It was sad, really. But, it was a blessing, too, because there came a point when I could no longer be around all those negative vibes. They were keeping me from what I really needed to do. I didn't want to quit outright, so I applied for a thirty-day leave.

"Are you really going to come back?" my supervisor asked me.

"Look at my face real good," I said. "The next time you see me, I'll be on TV."

I had seventeen dollars in the credit union.

I had seven dollars cash in my pocket.

Five of that seven dollars went to pay my cousin for the ride home from Frito-Lay.

That left two dollars cash, plus the seventeen in the credit union. Nineteen dollars to my name, and I had just walked away from my job.

On the way home, I got a page from Gary Williams. He wanted to know if I could start working at the Comedy Act on Friday and Saturday nights.

Being Large, Getting Big

I was raised to respect older people, but I hope when I'm old I don't get cantankerous, you know, like some of these old folks who figure it's their right to lip off to anybody, anytime. The truth is, now that I'm grown-up myself, I'm tired of old people saying what they want to say, and hurting your feelings, and then just walking off. As a child, I wasn't supposed to talk back to an older person. But I am an adult now, and I let their ass have it! I mean it. If you say something to me that hurts my feelings, I've got something for you. I was in church on a Sunday, and I spoke to this old woman, nice as I could be.

I said, "Hey, ma'am. How you doin'?"

She said, "Well, hey, baby. How big you gonna get?"

I said, "Well, bitch, how *old* you gonna get?"

We're in church now, do you understand? Now she's gonna ask me to take her home.

"Take me home, fat boy."

I said, "All right. Get in the car, you old bitch."

And if any of you all reading this don't like fat people, quit calling us names. We've heard them. And we don't give a damn. You want to make me mad, tell me Popeye's Chicken is going out of business. I'll set your house on fire.

You know you're a big man when you walk into a restaurant and you see the cook taking a deep breath. "Oh, damn, Lee, you ain't gonna believe this'un here, buddy. Come on out here and see this. Lord, I think I'm going to be needing a little help right now."

And these places have got to be kidding me with chicken wings. They bring you a plate of ten wings and say, "Enjoy!"

Enjoy? Damn, you better give me fifty and keep 'em cooking. You give me ten wings, and there's going to be a FIGHT! Unless they're turkey-wing size.

Have you ever gone to an all-you-can-eat restaurant and sat AT the buffet? I don't mean sit at a table BY the buffet, I mean sit AT the buffet. Right there by all the food. The manager said, "Y'all can't sit here!"

I said, "I don't see no sign! You have GOT to put a sign out if you don't want a brother to sit there."

I love those ladies in the supermarkets, standing at a table giving away food on toothpicks. I walked past those ladies twelve times, each time making faces like I'm some-body else. Come on, now, it's hard to get filled up on those little toothpick-sized portions! Finally, she starts eye-balling me as I'm coming by for the twelfth time.

"I seen you! You've been by before, you just making different faces every time."

"No, not me."

Baby James Brown

But she grabs that toothpick out of my hands. "I know who you are. Give me that damn toothpick!"

"But you can't let nobody eat it now!"

"Gimme it!"

And I'm standing there wrestling with this lady over a piece of cheddar cheese on the end of a toothpick! We crash to the ground, and she wants to throw that cube of cheese away before she's going to let me have it! I get ahold of it and swallow that cheese down, running like hell out of the store. Now, everyone at Kroger's sees me coming. I can't go into Kroger's anymore.

When you're big, one of the best things is when you can go to the mall and see somebody bigger than you are.

"Damn! I'm looking all right!"

But what you don't know is there's another big guy a little less big than you, right behind you going, "Damn!"

I have a cousin who is a little bit bigger than me. That fool went and bought a 1999 Ford Escort. He came out of the house and says, "Let's go get something to eat."

I said, "Damn, where am I gonna sit?"

He said, "I'll take the front, you get in the back."

I went with it. I said, "Dammit, let's ride."

We go by street corners, and everybody's leaning in to look, saying, "Man, look at all the people in that car!"

The police pulled us over. "All six of y'all, get outta the car! Oh, sorry, thought there was six of you in there. You go ahead and drive on."

I hate skinny people. I do. Another cousin of mine, he doesn't gain any weight at all. He'll be all up in my face with a Cinnabon, waving it around, going, "You can't eat this." I beat his ass down and eat it anyway.

Now I've been working with a trainer, and he's one of

109

these guys that doesn't think anybody is supposed to be fat. We'll be doing the repetitions and he'll scream at me, "Give me one more!"

I say, "You do one more. I'm tired. I want somethin' to eat."

He wants everyone to get up and eat oatmeal early in the morning.

Who wants to eat *oatmeal*?

You better give me some eggs and grits and about four pieces of that raisin toast!

Raisin toast! That's some serious stuff! I have to try and walk past raisin toast in the store with my eyes closed. I'll be in Atlanta shopping with my mother, and we'll be coming up on the raisin toast aisle. My mama says, "Close your eyes!"

And I say, "I can't, I can't! Help me, Jesus, resist the raisin toast!"

I swear, when I go out on stage, people look at me like they're worried I'm going to fall on them. And if I fall, who's going to pick me up? Nobody. Everybody will be standing across the street going, "That fat dude fell over there."

But I love being out on that stage. There is no denying it has brought a lot of blessings into my life. You never can tell who is out there enjoying what you do. I was fortunate enough to have met Stevie Wonder not too long ago. I was promoting one of my shows on the Los Angeles radio station that he owns, KJLH. It turns out, Stevie makes sure to drop by and see everybody that is appearing on his station. I told him it was good to see him, and he said, "It's good to be seen." He thanked me for being on the station. He told me he watches *Coming to the Stage*. Stevie Wonder is one blind man who, when he tells you he "watches" your show, you believe it. You know his eyes can't see, but let me tell you, brothers and sisters, he is looking right at you. He showed me his diamond watch, a watch that "counts" the time for him with clicks that click out the hour and the minutes. He rolled his head back and forth the way he does, and those big, happy teeth smiled at me, told me he liked what I was doing. I was thinking, "I hope I don't cry. I feel like I'm gonna start to cry." Not out of sadness, or pity, but love, for the spirit this man carried into the room with him. Thirty years after I met James Brown, and all I had to do this time was show up.

Showing up is it. I started showing up, getting out there at the Comedy Act. I just kept on. The toughest thing is starting to really believe in yourself. If you can get there, then you will start meeting people who believe in you, and can help you. It was my Atlanta boys Andre 3000 and Big Boi who came to see me do my comedy, and put me in the Outkast video for "So Fresh, So Clean." You know what? I did it for free. And things really started taking off for me after that. It got me out there in a way I couldn't have managed by myself. Andre and Big Boi, man, there are two different energies at work. Big Boi's tour bus is all about "let's get this party started." He's got the thumping bass going. There's a dancing pole in the damn bus. Andre's got violins and people wearing white gowns and all. But I've seen these two brothers pray together. It's a trip.

Then Too Short mentions me in "Shake That Monkey."
Skinny girls, let Bruce Bruce hit it!
And Lil Jon follows it up on "Salt Shaker."
Like Short said, let Bruce Bruce hit it!
It's love, all of that is love from these boys. Like when I pick guys out of my audience for the messed-up shirts they're wearing. It's love from Bruce Bruce!

But let me tell you something, black people will tell you when they don't like what you're doing. They don't even have to say anything. They'll just shake your hand after a show and then, real fast, they'll start talking to someone else.

"Hey, Bruce, great show man . . . *hey, LaWanda, how you doin', girl?*"

It's cold, but at least they're letting you know how they feel. Compared to how it works in show business, a snap like that from a fan is nothing. I've prepared this small chart below to tell you all you need to know about what it's like to move from Atlanta to Los Angeles.

THE BRUCE BRUCE GUIDE TO SHOW BUSINESS

WHAT THEY SAY	WHAT IT MEANS
"Not what we're looking for right now."	No.
"Give him another year."	No.
"Very good material."	No.
"There really isn't anyone out there doing what you do."	No.
"Love the suit."	No.
"I respect you, I understand your art, and I will do everything in my power to see that we have a long and fruitful creative partnership based on trust and mutual admiration."	No. For real.

Don't get me wrong, it's worth all the bullshit, I won't lie. But my life runs by a different set of rules now, and that has taken some getting used to.

When I ran up on James Brown back in the 1960s, I was a fan making myself known to a famous person. I was also a little boy at the time. Had I been an adult running up to James Brown and trying the same jive, here's how it would have gone down:

"Whoa! You're James Brown!"

"That's right."

"Hey, I'm thirty years old, and I do a great impression of you."

"Oh, damn."

"No, really, watch this! Hngh! Witchya bad self! Hngh! I'm black and I'm proud!"

"That's great. I will now have my bodyguard whoop your ass, you sad little man."

Seriously, what if one of your friends came up to you and said, "Hey, I do a great imitation of you, would you mind standing there while I act it out in front of you for a while?" You'd want to whoop their butt, too.

The thing is, when you have a little bit of celebrity, people think they know you. That's natural. You come into their lives on television, or in a comedy show, you're putting parts of yourself out there, and they're picking up on that. But in real life, you meet someone at a party, say, you start talking, you find things you have in common, you make a connection after a half an hour or so. Now, in the minds of some fans, because I give out so much information in my act, that connection has already happened. And I love the fact that I have fans. I wouldn't have been able to write this book if people weren't showing me love for what I do. But what you have to keep in mind is that, no matter how connected you think we are because of what I say on stage, I, myself, have never actually met your butt. With that in mind, here are some things to keep in mind around people who are in the public eye. Especially if the people in question are me.

1. Don't think you'll look like a fool if you, a grown man or woman, come at me for an autograph. First of all, it ain't dumb at all. It's nice, and as long as you get the time and place right, it's pretty simple. You find where I'm greeting folks after my show and say, "Hey, Bruce, can I have your autograph?"

2. Let's say you missed my show, but we end up in the same restaurant. Same guidelines as above, but what I ask here is that you *time* me. I notice you folks who are timing me, and I appreciate it. When you time me, you pay attention to where I'm at in the meal. I don't want to sign anything for you when my mouth is full of chicken or macaroni, or when I'm having my sweet tea refilled. Wait for a break in the action, and I'm happy to help.

3. However, DO NOT, I repeat, DO NOT send a little child to break the ice for you. I got real lucky doing my thing in front of James Brown because I was a boy. He indulged me. (Lucky for me, I also happened to do a dynamite James Brown.) Of course he indulged me. Who would not indulge a small child? You can't say no to a kid. It's emotional blackmail. So, if you take the extra consideration to time me at that restaurant, but then send a kid over instead of getting your butt up your own damn self, you have broken the unspoken covenant. Just letting you know. Unless you can prove it was the child's idea, then I might be down with it.

4. BRING YOUR OWN DAMN PEN.

5. Also, I do not like being asked to talk into somebody's cell phone. It happens a lot on escalators at airports, when I'm trapped on a slow-moving piece of machinery. Some dude in front of me will be talking on his cell phone, then he'll turn around and say, "Would you mind saying hello to my wife?" Now there's two ways I can go with that. One, a simple "And you are . . . ?" to the guy, or grabbing the phone and talking to the wife. "Heyyyy, bay-bay. Your narrow-butt husband has got to go. I hit a woman one time, I don't create nothing but stalkers."

6. Don't tell me you saw me on TV and thought I'd be taller. Nobody wants to hear that.

And people can flip on you! I was at a gas station in Atlanta, filling up the tank on my truck, running a little late to go and meet some friends at the airport. Now, the whole time I'm there, I see this lady at another pump is looking at me. I go up to the attendant to prepay, she's looking at me. I stand there pumping the gas, and she's looking at me. And by now I know she recognizes me. But she waits until I am through pumping gas, until I get into the truck, close the door, and turn the key before she walks up to me.

"Ain't you Bruce Bruce?"

"Yes, I am."

"Ain't you got no autographed pictures to give me or nothing?"

"I'm sorry, I was just heading out to pick somebody up at the airport, I don't have any—"

"Well. I didn't know you was so arrogant!" And she turns around and walks away. Do you believe that?

Truth is, most of you all know how to behave out there in the world, and you live by the same codes I do. And I can tell when a person is sincere, when they are expressing what comes from their heart. Lots of people come up to me and say, "I got a good joke for you, Bruce!" No harm in that. I usually tell them, "Hey, you trying to put me out of business?"

For real, these things that can get to you are only a small, small part of doing what I do. What I get most from folks is appreciation. Mostly what I hear is that people are getting something out of what I do. Somebody always tells me, "Man, I got an uncle just like that!" And when someone goes out of their way to tell me that before they saw my DVD or came to my show, they were having a hard day, but after they listened to my routine for an hour or so, their spirits got lifted, they felt like they could keep going. Well, that's nothing but a blessing, for them and for me.

I spend a lot of time on the road, and you might as well know right here, right now, I don't like to play around. I don't use the hotels I stay in for anything but sleeping. I'm really not any kind of party animal. I guess part of me is still that shy kid, that trash talker who really can't back it up. Plus, I'm more mature now. I have kids. I'm working hard. I've got a good relationship I don't need to mess with. Most important of all, though, I just hate getting used to a new woman. Fellas, you know what I mean? Man, you find yourself a woman that's good to you, that doesn't go crazy, that loves you for who you are, it's time you started realizing that's all there really is. It takes awhile to build that trust. And, like I said, you need that time, because you can be going awhile and sometimes you realize you still don't know a woman at all. People can flip on you, anytime, anywhere. Once you get that your woman is solid, that she is not going to flip, well, what the hell else do you want?

Now, by the same token, there are other ways to mess around on the road. I'm talking about goofing on people. When you travel so much, you have to find these childish ways of keeping everything fun, so you don't have time to think about how much you miss your woman, or your hometown. I play this game at hotel check-in desks where I rip on the clerks by pretending that I can't talk so good. I have to scope out the hotel as I'm walking up to the front desk, to see if there are two women on duty. It's not a sexist thing, it's just more fun. I may not be a player when I'm on the road, but I'm not going to get so desperate that I start flirting with men.

For a while, I was thinking of not putting this in the book, because then I knew I wouldn't be able to use it anymore, but what the hell, maybe now I'll be forced into coming up with something new. If this one were going to be in *Bruce Bruce: The Movie*, it would play like this:

INT. HOTEL—NIGHT

Bruce Bruce arrives at the hotel and steps up to the check-in desk. A pretty young female clerk stands behind the counter.

First female clerk
Can I help you, sir?

Bruce
(*pretending to stutter*)
Wi . . . Wi . . . Wi . . . Wi . . . Wi . . . sorry.

First female clerk
That's okay, sir.

Bruce
W . . . W . . . W . . . would you p-p-p-p-p—pull
up my reser- my reser- my reser- my reser-

First female clerk
Your reservation?

Bruce
That, that, that, that's right.

First female clerk
Under what name, sir?

Bruce
Br . . . Br . . . Br . . . Br . . . Br . . . Br . . . sorry.

First female clerk
Could you hold on a second, sir?
Bruce watches as the clerk ducks into the back room.
Bruce can hear her snorting with laughter, and asking her coworker to go out and deal with him.
After a moment, the second female clerk comes to the counter.

Second female clerk
May I help you, sir?

Bruce
(*suddenly shifts to a regular, very cultured voice*)
Yes, absolutely. I have a reservation under the name of
Bruce Bruce, and I would like a nonsmoking room, prefer-
ably a corner room, above the first floor, please, thank you
so much.

Second female clerk
All right. I can handle that for you. Would you wait just a
second, please?
Bruce waits as the second clerk ducks into the back room.
*He can hear them discussing something. It sounds like the
second clerk is trying to explain to the first clerk that there is
nothing wrong.*
*Suddenly, the first clerk comes back out and returns to the
counter.*

First female clerk
All right, sir, I'll process that room for you now.
The computer starts to feed out Bruce's paperwork.

Bruce
(*returning to his pretend stutter*)
Th . . . th . . . th . . . th . . . thank you.

First female clerk
Not a problem.

Bruce
Hey.

First female clerk
Yes, sir?

Bruce
You . . . you . . . you . . . you . . . you . . . you . . .

First female clerk
Take your time, sir.

Bruce
You . . . got a boyfriend?

First female clerk
I beg your pardon?

Bruce
I'm just rippin' on ya, baby.

First female clerk
Oh. I see.
Bruce now smiles. The clerk does not.

END OF SCENE

You have to keep it interesting, is all I'm saying.

Love

My uncle was there for me through thick and thin. He saw me through one of my early brushes with the heartache of unrequited love. It was my second-grade teacher, Miss Johnson. I loved that woman. I already figured I was her boyfriend, and I knew it wouldn't be long before I was going to marry her. It was the way she taught me how to spell. The way she taught me how to read. The way she said my name out loud every day, to make sure I was there. All right, so she did the same thing for every other damn kid in the classroom, but NOT THE SAME DAMN WAY, right? I could just tell; she had that different sound to her voice when she talked to me. She and I had a shared destiny. In second grade, I did not have a very clear picture of what that destiny was, or what the hell I could do with Miss Johnson when she did agree to marry me, but that didn't make those feelings any less real.

Then, one day, Miss Johnson asked me to wait a second after everyone had left the class. I thought she was ready to tell me that she understood how anxious I was to be her steady boyfriend, and that we could begin dating right away. Instead, she introduced me to a new world of hurt.

"You wanted to see me, Miss Johnson?"

"Bruce, isn't your uncle Paul a baker?" she asked me.

"Yeah, that's right."

"And he can make wedding cakes?"

"Sure he can. Who's getting married?"

"I am, Bruce. Me."

Up to that moment, in the seconds when I was anticipating the reason for Miss Johnson's wanting to talk to me, I had been singing "My Cherie Amour" in my head. Now, I could feel it ramping down, like someone had just switched the record from 45 to 16 rpm. *"Oh, cherie amour, prettttyyyy litttttttllle onnne thaaaaaat Iiiii adorrrrrrrrrr . . ."* (Anyone not old enough to remember records, you're out of luck with this description.)

"Is something the matter, Bruce?" I don't know how long I had been standing there with my head dropped back and my mouth half open, like I had just fallen asleep on a porch swing on a hot summer day.

"I . . . I . . . huh?" I said.

"I was asking if you think your uncle would like to make my wedding cake."

"Oh, uh . . ." I pulled myself together as best I could. "Sure," I said.

"Great. Tell him we'll stop by the house tonight to discuss the arrangements."

She was out the door before I could come out of my

stupor enough to think about what she just told me. *We'll stop by the house tonight.* Who was *we*? I wondered, even though I knew, somewhere in my second-grade soul, that *we* meant the man who was taking Miss Johnson away.

That night, she brought her fiancé over to talk with my uncle about their damn wedding cake.

"Thank you for meeting with us, Mr. Henson. Oh, hello, Bruce!"

She patted me on the head. The woman I loved went and *patted me on my damn head*! That's the kind of thing you do to a little boy!

I didn't say anything. I just watched the three adults go about their business. But every time that fiancé looked at me, I mean-mugged him till the cows came home. He must have thought I was some kind of devil child. After they left, my uncle stepped over to me.

"Bruce, what the hell was you mean-mugging that man all night for?"

"I don't like him."

"Why not?"

"Just because."

"That's no reason. Don't make me shoot up everybody in this house. I'll shoot everybody in this house and then give 'em a talking to if you don't tell me."

"Miss Johnson is kinda like my girlfriend."

"She's your girlfriend?"

"Yeah. I was supposed to marry her. Not that skunk."

"Aw, hell, Bruce," my uncle said. And then he knew, he just knew what I needed at that moment. He gave me the comfort I was looking for, as only he could. "You're talking about Miss Johnson, right?"

"Yeah."

"You like that ugly old dog? Man, that's the ugliest old woman I've ever seen!"

"She is?"

"That poor man is gonna marry that woman? Whoo-hoo, he's got a life of misery in store for him."

"He does?"

"That woman looked like a truck that got hit by another truck and lost the wreck."

I laughed. I was little, but I knew what he was doing. And if he hadn't taken care of me like that, I would never have been able to sit in Miss Johnson's classroom again without reliving all the pain a seven-year-old can muster. Thanks to my uncle's "ugly" jokes, I just looked at Miss Johnson, the prettiest lady I had ever seen, and laughed.

Now that I'm a grown man, I have learned one thing. And that one thing is that women are smooth. As smooth as any man out there. Women do fool around, just like men, but they don't get caught. Why?

When women fool around, they make sure the man lives across town, or out of town. Men will mess with next-door neighbors and coworkers, and wonder how the hell she found out.

And you will never catch a woman playing around on you. Or, if you do, you have to know somebody told on her. You didn't find out on your own. Because women have a plan. Then they have a backup plan. Then they have a backup plan to backup the backup plan. Women got it together. Women are thinking while you're asleep at night. You can go to sleep, and wake up at three in the morning, and there's your woman, looking right at you.

"Damn, woman, you ain't gone to sleep?"

"No . . . I'm thinking about something."

Women are smooth. That's why I need a woman who is down with me, and I mean down with me thoroughly. That means if we go somewhere together and we get into a fight, that means WE get into a fight. I don't need you hollering and screaming at me, I need you JABBING at me, baby!

I need a woman that will help me do ANYTHING. I don't care what it is. If I have to do a drive-by, she better be down with that. I want her to do the shooting.

Her: "Gimme that 9mm, sucka! Pull up, pull up, I got him!"

POW-POW!

Me: "Drive on, drive on!"

There's all kinds of jabbing, though, and women know what they can get away with. For example, maybe last night you made love to your woman and you finished too soon? She won't say anything that night, but she sure knows how to mess with you the next morning. You get up, head in to have breakfast, and she says, "Morning, *minute* man."

And you're thinking, "You better go on now, quit playing."

But she's ready with, "Kids! Breakfast will be ready in *just a minute*."

Now you say it out loud. "Real funny, girl, now you better quit playin'."

And she does quit. But not before she gets in one last one. "Get a move on, children, the school bus will be here in about *one minute*. Go on and ask your dad, he knows about that."

You have no choice here, fellas. You have to let her get **127** away with this to keep the peace, you understand? And she's worth it, because she's your woman, and she's good to you. So you have to get real good at knowing how to read her. You need to know the right thing to say, and the right time to say it, so that you aren't inviting unhappiness into your home. For example, if you pick your woman up from work, and she gets in the car and starts complaining about her job, "Oh, I'm so sick of this job, I just don't know what to do."

If you respond with, "Damn, girl, every time you get in this damn car, you're complaining about that damn job!" Brother, you are getting ready to have some difficulty in your house. What you need to do is just step back, and be cool. Do things differently.

So, now she gets into the car and says, "I'm so sick of this job, I just don't know what to do."

And you just say, "Hey, look, baby, don't worry. Everything's gonna be all right," and you give her a really sweet look. Get ready, because she's just going to be staring at you for a minute. Her eyes will be all wide, because it's going to take her a second to understand what just happened. Her man has been loving and supportive when she's feeling bad.

Then, she'll just look at you and say, "You want to get something to eat?"

And you'll say, "Hell, yeah, I want to get something to eat."

And she'll say, "Well, go on and stop at the store, then. Go ahead, baby."

Do you understand what I'm getting at here? Say you're working on your car, and you come inside to tell her, "Hey, baby, I'm working on the car, I'm gonna run down to Auto Zone, and I'll be right back."

She'll look at you all sweet and say, "Can I ride with you?"

And you say, "Damn! I said I'd be RIGHT BACK!" Once again, you are getting ready to bring misery into your relationship. But if you come back with, "Hey, baby, I'm working on the car, and I need to run down to Auto Zone, do you want to ride with me?"

And she'll get that sweet look again and say, "For real?"

And you take it even a step further with, "As a matter of fact, why don't you drive? Because I got all this oil on me."

As soon as you're over on the passenger side, she's on the driver's side so happy that she's bobbing her pretty head back and forth and singing a little song she just made up that goes something like:

"We're goin' to Auto Zone . . . we're goin' to Auto Zone, yeah . . ."

Basically, you need to have your woman MESSED UP MENTALLY. The way to do that is to be consistent with your woman on a day-to-day basis. Foreplay is very, very important in a relationship. A lot of men think foreplay is something you do before sex. They think foreplay is feeling on your girl, licking on her, then making love to her. Gentlemen, this is not foreplay. Foreplay is mental, and it is done twenty-four hours a day. And if you do this foreplay like I tell you to do it, and then you do make love to her, it won't take her very long to have an orgasm, because mentally . . . she's already there. But you have to be consistent on that day-to-day basis. Foreplay can mean numerous things. For example, if your woman finishes taking her shower and walks past you naked . . . pat that ass. She won't do anything but back up and present that behind for another one, going, "Boy, you better stop that!"

If your woman is in the kitchen cooking, walk up behind her like you're somebody else and say, "Hey, baby, you got a man?"

She's gonna say, "Damn, y'all know him, y'all know him . . ."

This is foreplay. And it's the little things that women like.

One thing I've learned is that if a woman loves you, she will do anything. But you have to get her to that point. A lot of you men are never getting her to that point because you never bond with your woman. And that's because a lot of you are already dealing with four or five women. And if you're dealing with four or five women, then I can sure as hell show you four or five women who are each *lacking something*. Because if you're doing the job right with one woman . . . you won't have TIME for another damn woman!

Don't forget now, part of doing the job right is making sure your personal hygiene is in order. If you're smelling like a bear, don't run up on a girl. And don't let your breath get stinky, all right? You can be sure, if your breath stinks, it will be a little kid that will tell you first.

You'll bend down to say hello to the child. "Hey, little girl—"

And she'll jump back! "Oooh! Is that your breath smelling like that? My mama said when your breath smells like that you got a lot of crap on your mind."

Nobody wants to talk to someone with bad breath. Have you ever smelled somebody's breath that's so bad you can *see* the words coming out of their mouth?

"Yeah, brother, I really SEE what you're talking about."

And sometimes you cannot hide your reaction to bad breath, but the other dude still does not get it. His mouth is right in front of you, and he's going, "Hhhhhhhow's your mama?"

And your eyes start blinking really fast. "Oh, she's fine."

"Why are you blinking like that?"

"I got something in my eye."

"Hhhhhhhow come every time I say something you move your head over to the side?"

"I, uh . . . I thought I saw somebody I knew behind you there."

Man, you can offer someone with bad breath a whole goddamn tin of Altoids, and they still won't get the hint. And fellas, if you're going to wear sandals, please get your feet done. You know what I'm talking about. Get that hard crap rubbed off your feet. Some of you right now are sleeping in socks because your feet are like bricks. They've got all sharp edges now. And then when you're sleeping with your girl and you kick out at night, you hit her across the leg with your nasty, crusty, hard feet.

She jumps up and starts screaming, "Get outta the bed, get outta the bed, something cut me on the leg!"

"What's wrong, baby?"

"I don't know what it is! Get outta the bed before it kills you, too!"

You know your feet are bad when you walk barefooted on the carpet and you pick a piece of carpet up with you.

BRUCE BRUCE

"Hey, what's wrong with that rug?"

"I believe it was them sticky-ass feet."

So maybe you have failed to follow Bruce Bruce's advice, and now you find yourself on your own again. No longer in a relationship. Have you noticed that when you break up with someone or get a divorce, a lot of your friends ask you why you didn't see it coming? Which only means that they spent however long you were together with this woman thinking to themselves, "That lady's insane," but they never bother to tell you that's what they've been thinking. But, even if they did, you probably wouldn't listen, and, let's face it, anyway, people hide some of the sides of their personality when they're just getting to know you. They put their best foot forward. And you're so horny, you're ready to believe that this woman has no faults. None. Zero.

My grandma used to say, "If you talk to someone long enough, you can figure out where they're coming from. You have to take the time to talk, but you have to know when to stop."

What she meant was, you have to look out for that point in the conversation when that conversation is done, and you have just heard all you need to hear. Here are a few examples:

1. **You:** So, you have a man?

   Her: Well . . .

   You: Yeah?

   Her: He's in jail right now.

THAT'S WHEN YOU KNOW TO STOP.

2. **You:** So, you have a man?

    Her: Not right now. The last boyfriend I had, he was cool until he got a little drunk at our Christmas party and I had to cuss him out in front of everyone.

    You: You cussed out your man in front of everybody?

    Her: Only until he started crying and ran out to the car.

THAT'S WHEN YOU KNOW TO STOP.

3. **You:** So, how many kids you have?

    Her: Nine.

AUTOMATIC STOP. BUT IF YOU THINK YOU CAN HANDLE IT, PRESS ON:

    You: Nine kids. How many baby daddies?

    Her: Nine.

DOUBLE AUTOMATIC STOP. ARE YOU FOOL ENOUGH TO CONTINUE?

    You: Nine baby daddies, huh?

    Her: Yeah.

    You: Uh-huh.

    Her: (*looks you straight in the eye*) I know we just met, but I really like you.

STOP! DAMN IT! STOP! GET THE HELL OUT OF THERE!

People get into relationships they had no business getting into. The signs were there, and all it took was a little moment to ask yourself, "Is this something I want to deal with?" Please, follow my advice. Bruce Bruce is looking out for you. He doesn't want you to have misery in your life. Don't ever be so hungry for pussy that you don't ask yourself these questions.

And women, I have not forgotten you. I know men are dogs, and you have to know when it's time for all talking to cease as well. Here's some examples. (Note: None of these are drawn from personal experience, mind you, just things I've heard about.)

1. **You:** I think I'm finally ready to marry and have children.

   Him: Me, too. Again.

TECHNICAL AUTOMATIC STOP, BUT IF YOU WANT TO, GO AHEAD:

   You: Again?

   Him: They say the sixth time is the charm.

STOP. FOR GOD'S SAKE, WOMAN, STOP.

2. **You:** I expect a man to take care of his obligations, but I'm also a career woman and believe in having an income of my own.

   Him: Fantastic. You buying?

AUTOMATIC STOP.

3. **You:** I can't be with a man who isn't monogamous.

Him: Who isn't what?

You: You don't know what "monogamous" means? Man, you're so stupid, you must have failed *Romper Room*.

Him: Wait a minute. Are you playing the dozens?

You: What, you saying women can't play the dozens?

Him: Who said I said that?

You: You think a woman shouldn't be cracking on you?

Him: Look, I don't know how this argument started . . .

You: Oh, now we're having an argument?

Him: It sure seems like it to me!

You: Oh, get the hell out.

Him: What?

You: Just go on, get!

Him: Fine! I'm gone!

Once again, ladies, these examples are based on independent laboratory studies conducted at the University of Georgia with a random sampling of women, and are not based on anything that Bruce Bruce himself has ever been involved with.

Why I Love The Andy Griffith Show

I used to think that only white people were racist. Like if a white person walks into a black nightclub, people will turn and look for a second, you know, "Check it out, a white guy just walked in," but that will be it, because they don't care. But if a brother walks into a redneck club, you can believe that twangy guitar music will STOP. Now, what they're thinking is, "Who the hell let him in here?" but most of them will say a couple of words to you, kind of quietly. For example, you say, "How you doin'?" and they say, "Pretty good." But you can tell the ones who really don't like black people by the way they don't answer your question. You step in and give one of them a "How you doin'?" and you get back a "Yup."

You know what that "yup" means? It means you get the hell out of there.

Now, when I grew up, prejudice was not allowed.

"People are with other people because it makes them

complete," my uncle would say. "There are certain things you just don't mess with. Hell, I may fall in love with a fat Chinese woman, and you better not tell me I can't!"

It made sense when my uncle said it, so I asked him, "Then how come black and white people are fighting all the time?"

"Because they're crazy, that's why." This was my uncle's response to all the questions about human nature that were too difficult to answer. "They're crazy." The thing is, he was right. When a mattress fell off the back of my truck on the highway, a hundred black faces blew on by in their cars, and it was a white guy who stopped to help me. You know Harriet Tubman had to have had some cool white folks helping her out along the way, and plenty of white folks got involved in civil rights back in the day.

I think, I hope, that kids today are getting that color doesn't matter, that there's good and bad in everyone. We've got Tiger Woods playing golf, admired by tons of white folks. We've got Eminem, a white rapper with a 90 percent black following. On my own TV show, *Coming to the Stage*, Greg Warren, a white comedian, was totally accepted by the audience. People are people and funny is funny.

I love Richard Pryor, and Redd Foxx and Moms Mabley and Eddie Murphy and Martin Lawrence.

I have also seen every episode of *The Andy Griffith Show* at least ten times. I can call out the lines everyone is going to say before they say them. *The Andy Griffith Show* is my all-time favorite television show, ever. I think *Soap* was the funniest, most groundbreaking show ever. *The Carol Burnett Show* was pure comedic genius. Milton Berle was hilarious.

You might say, "*The Andy Griffith Show*? You like that bunch of white crackers?" Hey, like my uncle said, I may fall in love with a fat Chinese woman. The characters on *Andy Griffith* are good people. You think good people don't exist? No one should be allowed to tell a story about the people who populate a town like Mayberry? I loved how Andy accepted Barney for the fool he was, and always tried to make him look good. I loved how Otis the drunk had a place in the town, and was taken care of despite his shortcomings. I loved how Opie was being raised without a mom, the way I got raised without a dad. I didn't give a damn about the color of their skin because what they were telling me was funny and universal. Flip Wilson had Andy Griffith on his show, and he had Redd Foxx on his show. My uncle's favorite show was *Sanford & Son*, but he loved *Gunsmoke* and *Hee Haw*, too. That's right, *Hee* freakin' *Haw*!

The whole damn thing comes down to good home training, good role models for how we treat other people and how we think about other people.

And I'm not saying there aren't some differences between the way black people behave and the way white people behave. In fact, there are exactly nine of them.

1. *White people are happy early in the morning*. They're all, "Good morning! . . . good morning, how are you? Lovely day, isn't it? Super! Good morning!"

Black people are not happy early in the morning. You catch a black person like that with a "Good morning, how are you?" and they'll give you, "Yeah, yeah . . . you just keep walking by, now. I mean it, leave me alone. Stop smilin' at me, damn it, I got a hangover, now LEAVE ME ALONE!"

2. *White people will fire your butt from a job and still be smiling.* Sometimes they'll even be giggling. I had a job once, the woman in personnel said to me, "I'm sorry, I've got to let you go-*ho-ho!*" "If you need a good reference, tell them to give me a ca-*ha-hall*. . . ."

I'm thinking, "Reference? Damn, I'm thinking about setting this place on fire."

When black people fire you, they ask you not to set the building on fire when you leave.

3. *White people let you know when something is going to happen.* If someone is behind me, getting ready to hit me on the head with a hammer, a white person is going to jump up and say, "Hey, watch yourself, buddy, he's going to hit you on the head with that hammer!" Then, I can turn around and catch the guy before he hits me.

Black people do not let you know when something is going to happen. Black people don't tell you anything! They'll talk among themselves, but they aren't going to say nothing to you. They'll just sit right there talking to their friend, "Look, he's going to hit him with that hammer . . . I think he's going to hit him . . . he's getting ready to hit him . . ."

And then *BAM!* You get hit in the head with the hammer, and they say, "See, I told you so. I told you that guy was going to hit him on the head, didn't I tell you?"

4. *White people usually pay you back on time.* A white person writes you a check, you can take it to the bank in the morning.

Black people don't usually pay you back on time. A brother writes you a check, he's going to postdate it next Friday. He'll look you straight in the eye and say, "I'm telling you, if you go in there Thursday, ain't no money gonna be there for you." And black people have got some messed-up credit, don't we? Every time we run that card through, right as we're swiping it, we call out, "In the name of Jesus, Father, God, please let that card go through, hallelujah!" Back in the day they had that big old metal bar that went *click-click* over your card, and you didn't have to worry for a couple of weeks about whether you had it covered or not. Nowadays, you better ask Jesus to put the whammy on the damn computer.

5. *White people say, "For the love of God" when something crazy happens.*

Black people say, "Jesus," when something crazy happens. Because we know there is power in that name, "Jesus." If you're driving, and your car starts suddenly sliding around, a black person will say, "Jesus, car! Straighten up!" See, that's a request. That's asking for help. The white person's car starts sliding around and it will go like this:

"For the love of—" *WHAM!* So, white people, start calling out "Jesus," it will work for you.

6. *White people make deals with their children.* (See page 73.)

Black people do not make deals with their children. (See page 73.)

7. *White people come right up on strangers' dogs.* They will see a stranger coming at them with a dog that they don't know, and they will go right up to the damn thing.

Black people are already crossing the street. They're just a little smarter than white people in that regard.

8. *White people say "stark naked."*

Black people say "butt naked." In the neighborhood, if a wife catches her husband with another woman, and she puts him out on the street naked, then the police come by and ask the neighbors what happened. They say, "Man, when she pushed him out that door, he was butt naked."

But if this happens to a white person, the police ask the neighbor what happened, and he says, "My goodness, I couldn't believe it when I saw it. When she pushed that man outside, the sumbitch was stark naked."

What is stark naked?

9. *White people always get drunker than something.*

Black people just get drunk. Ask a black man if he's drunk, he'll tell you, "Drunk? Man, I am messed up."

Ask a white guy, "Are you drunk?" He'll tell you, "Drunk? I'm drunker'n Cootie Brown!"

Who the hell is Cootie Brown?

And that's pretty much it. Only nine differences between black and white people! Amazing, isn't it? These are cultural differences, differences that come out of behavior. But the way people feel, the things they're going through in their hearts? No difference there. More people have to know that as time goes on, is all.

I remember watching the TV news in Georgia in 1987, when Hosea Williams led a protest march into all-white Forsyth County. That man called the whole nation's attention to the Ku Klux Klan presence in Forsyth. Hosea, who passed away in 2000, was a great African-American leader. He served in an all-black unit attached to General Patton's Third Army in World War II. He worked closely with Martin Luther King, and he led the march on Selma that became a turning point for the rights of black people in this country. The first time he marched on Forsyth, in 1987, he had seventy-five people alongside him. They were all assaulted by members of the Klan. The very next week, he led another march, with twenty thousand people, and then no one could ignore them.

While I was watching the TV coverage of this event, I saw a white man from Forsyth being interviewed about Hosea Williams's plans to march there. The white man looked angry and threatening. He said, "Hosea Williams can come up here if he wants, but if we catch him after dark, it's time to play." That's some scary, ugly crap.

And the man was holding a baby in his arms.

That really got to me, because I saw it pretty clearly then. That white man in Forsyth got that way of being, that hate, from *his* home training. That was the message he got. And that means he was giving the same message to the little baby in his arms. That man believed that hatred was the way to go, because no one had told him any different. He was taught to reject everything just like I was taught to accept everything. It's as simple as that. And maybe one day he, or that little baby, will get a little older and meet someone who can set them straight. Someone who can help them see that, like my uncle said, they've been crazy. It happens.

The Last Page

When I do my stand-up act, I don't have a closing joke, because, like I said when we started, I don't tell jokes. I tell real life stories. You will find most comedians have some kind of big joke they use to end the show, so they can call out, "Peace! I'm outta here!" But I don't do that. So, when I get through performing, I just get the hell off the stage.

And now that I'm through writing this book, I will just get the hell off the page.

About the Author

Bruce Bruce is a name synonymous with keeping audiences rolling with laughter thanks to his captivating improv skills. Bruce's larger-than-life comedic style has been showcased across the country as well as on hit television programs, while his wit, spontaneity, and dazzling personality set him apart from other stand-up comedians. Although Bruce is known for his adult comedy, he prides himself on not using vulgarity to win a laugh. He also does comedy appropriate for the entire family, and has earned his title as the "Mayor of Comedy." After receiving the highest ratings ever as the host of BET's *Comic View* for two seasons, Bruce returned to the BET family this past October, as the new host of the highly rated *Coming to the Stage*.

Bruce starred in his own *Comedy Central Presents* special early last year, and Urban Works Entertainment released a one-hour comedy special DVD *Bruce Bruce Live* this past summer. Bruce can be seen in Ice Cube's "XXX: State of the Union," and in a cameo role as "Lime Pimp" in *Hair Show*, starring Mo'Nique and Kellita Smith. He also recently shot a role in *Cloud Nine*, starring D. L. Hughley. Bruce was named the most recent host of *Original Kings of Comedy* promoter Walter Latham's last comedy tour, the Crown Royal Comedy Festival. He has made guest appearances in videos with Ludacris and the Ying Yang Twins (after being referred to by name in their hit song "Salt Shaker"). He appeared in the monstrous 1996 summer hit "Come On Ride the Train (Ride It)" by Quad City DJs, and can also be seen in Outkast's music video "So Fresh, So Clean." And he is featured alongside Dr. Dre and Snoop Dogg in the Lions Gate Films' feature *The Wash*.

When not performing in comedy clubs across the country, Bruce divides his time between his homes in Atlanta and Los Angeles. He is also extremely dedicated to his incredible car collection, which includes two Harley-Davidson trucks and four Buick muscle cars, among others.

About the CD

The attached CD was recorded live at Tommy T's Comedy House in Concord, California, on May 7, 2005. Many thanks to David Bentley, Don Shaw, and the entire staff of Tommy T's for their cooperation; to Kevin McKereghan and BBI Engineering Inc. for recording the performance; and to Matt Teacher and Sine Studios for creating the CD.

Other Products

For more information about Bruce Bruce, including upcoming appearances, DVDs, and other merchandise, please visit his Web site at www.bruce-bruce.com.